CHARTA OECUMENICA

CHARTA OECUMENICA

A Text, a Process and a Dream of the Churches in Europe

Edited by
Viorel Ionita and Sarah Numico

WCC Publications, Geneva

Conference of European Churches (CEC)
Conférence des Eglises européennes (KEK)
Konferenz Europäischer Kirchen (KEK)

P.O. Box 2100 – 150, route de Ferney
CH-1211 Geneva 2, Switzerland
Tel: +41 22 791 61 11 Fax: +41 22 791 62 27
E-mail: cec@cec-kek.org Home-page: www.cec-kek.org

Consilium Conferentiarum Episcoporum Europae (CCEE)
Council of European Bishops' Conferences (CCEE)
Rat der Europäischen Bischofskonferenzen (CCEE)
Conseil des Conférences Episcopales Européennes (CCEE)

Gallusstrasse, 24
CH - 9000 St. Gallen
Tel: +41 71 227 33 74 Fax: +41 71 227 33 75
E-mail: ccee@ccee.ch Home-page: www.ccee.ch

Cover design: Viorel Ionita and Lucian Sacrieru

ISBN: 2-8254-1385-2

Printed in Romania

Table of Contents

Introduction

Almost two years after the signing of the *Charta Oecumenica - Guidelines for the Growing Cooperation among the Churches in Europe*, the secretariats of the Council of European Bishops' Conferences (CCEE) and the Conference of European Churches (CEC) are pleased to present to the churches, communities and all interested persons this work, which recounts the early phases in the *Charta* process.

The book contains articles by persons who have been witnesses to this adventure which is still going on. They tell of the principal stages in the story of the *Charta,* and the new experiences now taking place in Europe arising from this initiative by the churches and communities on this continent.

The book begins with the text of the *Charta Oecumenica - Guidelines for the Growing Cooperation among the Churches in Europe.* Following the version which was signed and distributed on 22 April 2001, there was a new edition of the text in which a few errors were corrected which had appeared progressively in the course of translation from the original German. These were mainly editorial corrections.

The article by CCEE General Secretary Aldo Giordano, "Why a European *Charta Oecumenica?*" places the *Charta* in the ecumenical context of our continent today.

It is Viorel Ionita, CEC Study Secretary, who recounts the "origin" of the *Charta*, that is, the process of drawing up the text, which took about four years, from the Second European Ecumenical Assembly in Graz, 1997, to the Ecumenical European Encounter in Strasbourg which began the millennium, entitled "I am with you always...", where the text was officially signed on 22 April 2001. "The signing of the *Charta*", a contribution by the two voices of Viorel Ionita (CEC Study Secretary) and Sarah Numico (CCEE press officer), provides a detailed chronicle of the Strasbourg event, enriched by some brief reflections.

Then come presentations on the three main chapters of the *Charta*, theological and spiritual readings of its significance. In Part I, "We believe in one holy catholic and apostolic church", we hear from an Orthodox theologian, Grigorios Larentzakis; Part II, "On the way towards the visible fellowship of the churches in Europe", is analysed by a Catholic theologian, Waclaw Hryniewicz, while a Protestant theologian, Reinhard Frieling, gives his reading of Part III, "Our common responsibility in Europe".

The article on "Testimonies and experiences from the life of the *Charta*" by Sarah Numico provides a taste of the events which we have witnessed in the CCEE and CEC secretariats, in the awareness that the initiatives taken by churches at the local level are infinitely more numerous and varied than those which we are able to pass on to you ourselves.

The three contributions which follow offer a wider view: from "The young protagonists", by Petra Paidakovic, a youth delegate from Croatia to the Ecumenical European Encounter in Strasbourg; on "The contribution of the Charta Oecumenica to European construction" by Keith Jenkins, former director of CEC's Church and Society Commission, and John Coughlan, Episcopal Commission of the European Community (COMECE); and "The challenge of interreligious dialogue" by Heinz Klautke and Hans Vöcking, Co-Moderators of the CEC-CCEE Committee "Islam in Europe".

Finally, the text by Keith Clements, CEC General Secretary, proposes "Prospects for the future" of the continuing *Charta* process and the ecumenical journey of the churches of Europe.

We are aware that it is not possible to tell the whole story of what is being done in Europe as a result of the *Charta* and thanks to it. What is here recounted is seen from the point of view of the CCEE and CEC secretariats. Every local church and every community which has received the text could write its own "story of the *Charta Oecumenica*"; on the way, it has perceived the text, experienced it and shared it at the local level.

The course which the *Charta Oecumenica* has taken is amazing in various ways, but certainly has only now begun. We have faith that this young seedling, which is entering by degrees into the ecumenical programme of numerous churches in Europe, is destined to be an important instrument for the churches' path towards unity, promoting tangible commitments by the new ecumenical population which has been appearing almost everywhere in Europe in these last few years. It is our hope that this book will stimulate new ideas and new projects!

Although this book is published by our two secretariats, it is clear that we do not pretend to offer here the official views of CCEE and CEC. The authors of the various chapters retain the authority and the responsibility for their contributions. We here express our warm thanks to them, as well as to all those involved in editing the book for publication and to the translators who helped to prepare the texts in French, German, Italian and English.

To our Father in heaven we commit our work, and the future of the *Charta Oecumenica*, with our fervently renewed prayers that the kingdom of God may soon come, and that Christians may welcome the gift of unity.

Amédée Grab, Bishop of Chur, President of CCEE
Jérémie, Metropolitan of Switzerland, President of CEC

Bucharest, January 2003

CHARTA OECUMENICA

CHARTA OECUMENICA

CARTA OECUMENICA
Guidelines for the Growing Cooperation among the Churches in Europe

Glory be to the Father, and to the Son, and to the Holy Spirit

As the Conference of European Churches (CEC) and the Council of European Bishops' Conferences (CCEE)1 we are, in the spirit of the Messages from the two European Ecumenical Assemblies of Basle (1989) and Graz (1997), firmly resolved to preserve and develop the fellowship that has grown up among us. We give thanks to the Triune God for guiding our steps towards an ever deeper fellowship through the Holy Spirit.

Various forms of ecumenical co-operation have already proved themselves. Christ's prayer is: "...that they may all be one. As you, Father, are in me and I am in you, may they also be in us, so that the world may believe that you have sent me" (John 17:21). If we are to be faithful to this prayer, we cannot be content with the present situation. Instead, aware of our guilt and ready to repent, we must strive to overcome the divisions still existing among us, so that together we may credibly proclaim the message of the Gospel among all people.

Listening together to God's word in Holy Scripture, challenged to confess our common faith and to act together in accordance with the perceived truth, let us bear witness to the love and hope which are for all people.

---

[1] *To the Conference of European Churches (CEC) belong almost all Orthodox, Protestant, Anglican, Old-Catholic and independent churches in Europe. In the Council of European Bishops' Conferences (CCEE) are represented all Roman Catholic Bishops' Conferences in Europe.*

Europe - from the Atlantic to the Urals, from the North Cape to the Mediterranean - is today more pluralist in culture than ever before. With the Gospel, we want to stand up for the dignity of the human person created in God's image and, as churches together, contribute towards reconciling peoples and cultures.

In this spirit, we adopt this charter as a common commitment to dialogue and co-operation. It describes fundamental ecumenical responsibilities, from which follow a number of guidelines and commitments. It is designed to promote an ecumenical culture of dialogue and co-operation at all levels of church life, and to provide agreed criteria for this. However, it has no magisterial or dogmatic character, nor is it legally binding under church law. Its authority will derive from the voluntary commitments of the European churches and ecumenical organisations. Building on this basic text, they can formulate their own local addenda, designed to meet their own specific challenges and resulting commitments.

I. WE BELIEVE IN
"ONE HOLY CATHOLIC AND APOSTOLIC CHURCH"

"(Make) every effort to maintain the unity of the Spirit in the bond of peace. There is one body and one Spirit, just as you were called to the one hope of your calling, one Lord, one faith, one baptism, one God and Father of all, who is above all and through all and in all" (Ephesians 4:3-6)

1. Called Together to Unity in Faith

With the Gospel of Jesus Christ, according to the witness of Holy Scripture and as expressed in the ecumenical Nicene-Constantinopolitan Creed of 381, we believe in the Triune God: the Father, Son and Holy Spirit. Because we here confess "one, holy, catholic and apostolic church" our paramount ecumenical task is to show forth this unity, which is always a gift of God.

Fundamental differences in faith are still barriers to visible unity. There are different views of the church and its oneness, of the sacraments and ministries. We must not be satisfied with this situation. Jesus Christ revealed to us on the cross his love and the mystery of reconciliation; as his followers, we intend to do our utmost to overcome the problems and obstacles that still divide the churches.

We commit ourselves

- to follow the apostolic exhortation of the Letter to the Ephesians and persevere in seeking a common understanding of Christ's message of salvation in the Gospel;

- in the power of the Holy Spirit, to work towards the visible unity of the Church of Jesus Christ in the one faith, expressed in the mutual recognition of baptism and in eucharistic fellowship, as well as in common witness and service.

II. ON THE WAY TOWARDS THE VISIBLE FELLOWSHIP OF THE CHURCHES IN EUROPE

"By this everyone will know that you are my disciples, if you have love for one another" (John 13:35)

2. Proclaiming the Gospel together

The most important task of the churches in Europe is the common proclamation of the Gospel, in both word and deed, for the salvation of all. The widespread lack of corporate and individual orientation and falling away from Christian values challenge Christians to testify to their faith, particularly in response to the quest for meaning which is being pursued in so many forms. This witness will require increased dedication to Christian education (e.g. catechism classes) and pastoral care in local congregations, with a sharing of experiences in these fields. It is equally important for the whole people of God together to communicate the Gospel in the public domain, which also means responsible commitments to social and political issues.

We commit ourselves

- to discuss our plans for evangelisation with other churches, entering into agreements with them and thus avoiding harmful competition and the risk of fresh divisions;

- to recognise that every person can freely choose his or her religious and church affiliation as a matter of conscience, which means not inducing anyone to convert through moral pressure or material incentive, but also not hindering anyone from entering into conversion of his or her own free will.

3. Moving towards one another

In the spirit of the Gospel, we must reappraise together the history of the Christian churches, which has been marked by many beneficial experiences but also by schisms, hostilities and even armed conflicts. Human guilt, lack of love and the frequent abuse of faith and the church for political interests have severely damaged the credibility of the Christian witness.

Ecumenism therefore begins for Christians with the renewal of our hearts and the willingness to repent and change our ways. The ecumenical movement has already helped to spread reconciliation.

It is important to acknowledge the spiritual riches of the different Christian traditions, to learn from one another and so to receive these gifts. For the ecumenical movement to flourish it is particularly necessary to integrate the experiences and expectations of young people and actively encourage their participation.

We commit ourselves
- to overcome the feeling of self-sufficiency within each church, and to eliminate prejudices; to seek mutual encounters and to be available to help one another;
- to promote ecumenical openness and co-operation in Christian education, and in theological training, continuing education and research.

4. Acting together

Various forms of shared activity are already ecumenical. Many Christians from different churches live side by side and interact in friendships, in their neighbourhoods, at work and in their families. Couples in interdenominational marriages especially should be supported in experiencing ecumenism in their daily lives.

We recommend that bilateral and multilateral ecumenical bodies be set up and maintained for co-operation at local, regional, national and international levels. At the European level it is necessary to strengthen co-

10

operation between the Conference of European Churches and the Council of European Bishops' Conferences (CCEE) and to hold further European Ecumenical Assemblies.

In the event of conflicts between churches, efforts towards mediation and peace should be initiated and/or supported as needed.

We commit ourselves
- to act together at all levels of church life wherever conditions permit and there are no reasons of faith or overriding expediency mitigating against this;
- to defend the rights of minorities and to help reduce misunderstandings and prejudices between majority and minority churches in our countries.

5. Praying together

The ecumenical movement lives from our hearing God's word and letting the Holy Spirit work in us and through us. In the power of this grace, many different initiatives now seek, through services of prayer and worship, to deepen the spiritual fellowship among the churches and to pray for the visible unity of Christ's Church. A particularly painful sign of the divisions among many Christian churches is the lack of eucharistic fellowship.

In some churches reservations subsist regarding praying together in an ecumenical context. But we have many hymns and liturgical prayers in common, notably the Lord's Prayer, and ecumenical services have become a widespread practice: all of these are features of our Christian spirituality.

We commit ourselves
- to pray for one another and for Christian unity;
- to learn to know and appreciate the worship and other forms of spiritual life practised by other churches;
- to move towards the goal of eucharistic fellowship.

6. Continuing in dialogue

We belong together in Christ, and this is of fundamental significance in the face of our differing theological and ethical positions. Rather than seeing our diversity as a gift which enriches us, however, we have allowed differences of opinion on doctrine, ethics and church law to lead to separations between churches, with special historical circumstances and different cultural backgrounds often playing a crucial role.

In order to deepen ecumenical fellowship, endeavours to reach a consensus in faith must be continued at all cost. Only in this way can church communion be given a theological foundation. There is no alternative to dialogue.

We commit ourselves
- to continue in conscientious, intensive dialogue at different levels between our churches, and to examine the question of how official church bodies can receive and implement the findings gained in dialogue;
- in the event of controversies, particularly when divisions threaten in questions of faith and ethics, to seek dialogue and discuss the issues together in the light of the Gospel.

III. OUR COMMON RESPONSIBILITY IN EUROPE

"Blessed are the peacemakers, for they will be called children of God" (Matthew 5:9)

7. Participating in the building of Europe

Through the centuries Europe has developed a primarily Christian character in religious and cultural terms. However, Christians have failed to prevent suffering and destruction from being inflicted by Europeans, both within Europe and beyond. We confess our share of responsibility for this guilt and ask God and our fellow human beings for forgiveness.

Our faith helps us to learn from the past, and to make our Christian faith and love for our neighbours a source of hope for morality and ethics, for education and culture, and for political and economic life, in Europe and throughout the world.

The churches support an integration of the European continent. Without common values, unity cannot endure. We are convinced that the spiritual heritage of Christianity constitutes an empowering source of inspiration and enrichment for Europe. On the basis of our Christian faith, we work towards a humane, socially conscious Europe, in which human rights and the basic values of peace, justice, freedom, tolerance, participation and solidarity prevail. We likewise insist on the reverence for life, the value of marriage and the family, the preferential option for the poor, the readiness to forgive, and in all things compassion.

As churches and as international communities we have to counteract the danger of Europe developing into an integrated West and a disintegrated East, and also take account of the North-South divide within Europe. At the same time we must avoid Eurocentricity and heighten Europe's sense of responsibility for the whole of humanity, particularly for the poor all over the world.

We commit ourselves
- to seek agreement with one another on the substance and goals of our social responsibility, and to represent in concert, as far as possible, the concerns and visions of the churches vis-à-vis the secular European institutions;
- to defend basic values against infringements of every kind;
- to resist any attempt to misuse religion and the church for ethnic or nationalist purposes.

8. Reconciling peoples and cultures

We consider the diversity of our regional, national, cultural and religious traditions to be enriching for Europe. In view of numerous conflicts, the churches are called upon to serve together the cause of reconciliation among peoples and cultures. We know that peace among the churches is an important prerequisite for this.

Our common endeavours are devoted to evaluating, and helping to resolve, political and social issues in the spirit of the Gospel. Because we value the person and dignity of every individual as made in the image of God, we defend the absolutely equal value of all human beings.

As churches we intend to join forces in promoting the process of democratisation in Europe. We commit ourselves to work for structures of peace, based on the non-violent resolution of conflicts. We condemn any form of violence against the human person, particularly against women and children.

Reconciliation involves promoting social justice within and among all peoples; above all, this means closing the gap between rich and poor and overcoming unemployment. Together we will do our part towards giving migrants, refugees and asylum-seekers a humane reception in Europe.

We commit ourselves
- to counteract any form of nationalism which leads to the oppression of other peoples and national minorities and to engage ourselves for non-violent resolutions;
- to strengthen the position and equal rights of women in all areas of life, and to foster partnership in church and society between women and men.

9. Safeguarding the creation

Believing in the love of the Creator God, we give thanks for the gift of creation and the great value and beauty of nature. However, we are appalled to see natural resources being exploited without regard for their intrinsic value or consideration of their limits, and without regard for the well-being of future generations.

Together we want to help create sustainable living conditions for the whole of creation. It is our responsibility before God to put into effect common criteria for distinguishing between what human beings are scientifically and technologically capable of doing and what, ethically speaking, they should not do.

We recommend the introduction in European churches of an Ecumenical Day of Prayer for the Preservation of Creation.

We commit ourselves
- to strive to adopt a lifestyle free of economic pressures and consumerism and a quality of life informed by accountability and sustainability;
- to support church environmental organisations and ecumenical networks in their efforts for the safeguarding of creation.

10. Strengthening community with Judaism

We are bound up in a unique community with the people Israel, the people of the Covenant which God has never terminated. Our faith teaches us that our Jewish sisters and brothers "are beloved, for the sake of their ancestors; for the gifts and the calling of God are irrevocable" (Rom 11.28-29). And "to them belong the adoption, the glory, the covenants, the giving of the law, the worship and the promises; to them belong the patriarchs, and from them, according to the flesh, comes the Messiah" (Rom 9.4-5).

We deplore and condemn all manifestations of anti-Semitism, all outbreaks of hatred and persecutions. We ask God for forgiveness for anti-Jewish attitudes among Christians, and we ask our Jewish sisters and brothers for reconciliation.

It is urgently necessary, in the worship and teaching, doctrine and life of our churches, to raise awareness of the deep bond existing between the Christian faith and Judaism, and to support Christian-Jewish co-operation.

We commit ourselves

- to oppose all forms of anti-Semitism and anti-Judaism in the church and in society;

- to seek and intensify dialogue with our Jewish sisters and brothers at all levels.

11. Cultivating relations with Islam

Muslims have lived in Europe for centuries. In some European countries they constitute strong minorities. While there have been plenty of good contacts and neighbourly relations between Muslims and Christians, and this remains the case, there are still strong reservations and prejudices on both sides. These are rooted in painful experiences throughout history and in the recent past.

We would like to intensify encounters between Christians and Muslims and enhance Christian-Islamic dialogue at all levels. We recommend, in particular, speaking with one another about our faith in one God, and clarifying ideas on human rights.

We commit ourselves
- to conduct ourselves towards Muslims with respect;
- to work together with Muslims on matters of common concern.

12. Encountering other religions and world views

The plurality of religious and non-confessional beliefs and ways of life has become a feature of European culture. Eastern religions and new religious communities are spreading and also attracting the interest of many Christians. In addition, growing numbers of people reject the Christian faith, are indifferent to it or have other philosophies of life.

We want to take seriously the critical questions of others, and try together to conduct fair discussions with them. Yet a distinction must be made between the communities with which dialogues and encounters are to be sought, and those which should be warned against from the Christian standpoint.

We commit ourselves

- to recognise the freedom of religion and conscience of these individuals and communities and to defend their right to practise their faith or convictions, whether singly or in groups, privately or publicly, in the context of rights applicable to all;

- to be open to dialogue with all persons of good will, to pursue with them matters of common concern, and to bring a witness of our Christian faith to them.

*

Jesus Christ, the Lord of the one Church, is our greatest hope of reconciliation and peace.

In his name we intend to continue on our common path in Europe. We pray for God's guidance through the power of the Holy Spirit.

"May the God of hope fill us with all joy and peace in believing, so that we may abound in hope by the power of the Holy Spirit." (Rom 15.13)

As Presidents of the Conference of European Churches and the Council of European Bishops' Conferences, we commend this Charta Oecumenica as a Basic Text to all the churches and Bishops' Conferences in Europe, to be adopted and adapted in each of their local contexts.

With this commendation we hereby sign the Charta Oecumenica, on the occasion of the European Ecumenical Encounter, on the first Sunday after the common celebration of Easter in the year 2001.

Strasbourg, 22 April 2001

Metropolitan Jérémie
President Conference
of European Churches

Cardinal Vlk
President Council of
European Bishops' Conferences

16

I. THE HISTORY OF THE CHARTA OECUMENICA

Why a *Charta Oecumenica* for Europe?

Aldo Giordano

When we came out of St. Thomas' Church in Strasbourg on 22 April 2001, after the CCEE and CEC Presidents had just signed the Charta Oecumenica, an Orthodox metropolitan said to me, "Look, there's a bit of blue sky up there, after it's been cloudy all these days; a sign that God is blessing our endeavour!" In travelling the roads of Europe, one often has the impression that the sky is closed or that there is a lack of fresh air to breathe. The Charta Oecumenica is a text, a process and a dream, all at the same time; it dreams of contributing to uncovering the blue sky again over Europe and its churches. It aims to bring the Christians of our countries to rediscover their vocation and their responsibility for reconciliation.

I am realising more and more that every project or initiative of the church is weighty with life, with communion, prayer and suffering. The Charta is already the fruit of a task undertaken together, of dialogues, of efforts and hopes. When we in the CCEE secretariat began receiving, from all over Europe, letters, messages and telephone calls from various persons, monastic communities, religious families, dioceses, parishes and movements, telling us "We are praying and doing everything we can now for the Ecumenical Encounter in Strasbourg and the Charta Oecumenica process," or "We are organising meetings at the local level to share our thoughts about the Charta and to make concrete plans," we were certain that God had blessed the Encounter, and that the Charta would bear fruit because it is God's gift, beyond all our limitations and in spite of all our sins.

1. The urgency of reconciliation

The historical situation in which we find ourselves, since the tragedy of 11 September in the United States and the new threat of war, has

19

revealed once again the serious responsibility which Christians have, the urgency of reconciliation and restoring visible unity among churches and church communities. The divisions among Christians, after all, are obstacles to proclaiming that life according to the Gospel which can bring about universal brotherhood and sisterhood and true alternatives to violence, injustice and terrorism.

European history bears witness to the serious political and cultural consequences of the divisions among Christians. It can be said that the many religious wars which have broken out here have forced the culture and the society to distance themselves from their direct inspiration by the Christian faith and to take other paths. The believers who were the originators of modern thought, such as Descartes, Grozio or Kant, used points of reference other than the Gospel, and a more autonomous concept of reason, in order to find a common, acceptable ground on which to found philosophy, law and a sustainable peace.

But the challenges facing Europe today are calling the churches and Christian communities to turn over a new page in the history of unity. How shall we help to build a "European home" which shelters our diverse peoples, cultures, ethnicities and religions, without annihilating their distinctive identities through totalitarian systems on one hand, or falling into conflicts which destroy differences, or into terrorism, on the other? How shall we as Europeans fulfil our responsibility for the problems of the rest of humanity, especially the southern hemisphere, through a logic of sharing of gifts? How shall we be present as churches in a society characterised by cultural, ethical and religious pluralism? How shall we together approach the great ethical questions which are being put to humankind, from biomedicine to peace and ecology? How shall we respond to the profound search for meaning, for love, for happiness, which is being felt anew and even more sharply in this post-ideological Europe, especially among the younger generation, and in particular with regard to experiences of suffering and death?

The Charta Oecumenica results from the awareness that the churches have no credible answer to these problems if they are not able to regain a consensus and unity amongst themselves. It is especially when visiting the European institutions in Brussels or Strasbourg that I realise how heavily the divisions among Christians weigh upon the future of Europe. How can the churches contribute to European unity if they are divided from one another? Can one even imagine a united Europe with the churches still divided? Moreover, Europe is the very continent which has exported the divisions it created at home to other regions of the world. Now it is time for us to export the reconciliation we have rediscovered.

The Charta is, furthermore, a part of the current ecumenical situation in Europe. Since the fall of the Berlin wall, the fundamental ecumenical problem seems to be that of relations between the cultures and traditions of East and West. Some painful issues, such as that of proselytism, or of relations between Orthodox and Greek Catholic churches, or the recent debates between Orthodox and Protestant churches within the ecumenical organisations, go back to this encounter between the Latin and Eastern traditions. Many classic ecumenical debates, such as those on the ordained ministry, eucharistic hospitality, the primacy of the pope, Mariology, ethical questions and so forth, are also marked by the relations between the East and modern (or postmodern) European culture. Behind many current difficulties is the fear experienced by the East of giving in to Western culture, which is seen as pluralist, secular and relativist and threatens to undermine the Eastern tradition. It seems to me that the most serious "ecumenical" contribution which might bring some light into this new situation would be to commit ourselves to the new form of evangelisation which we have been talking about for years. If the churches succeeded in making it understood that the Gospel can dialogue with every culture, including that of the West, and has the power to "convert" every type of culture, many of the fears of the Eastern churches would subside.

But other voices must also be given more room in the ecumenical scene: those of the free churches, the Pentecostals, the charismatics, those from the southern hemisphere and other regions of the earth, such as Africa, Asia or Latin America, who often feel that our debates are very far removed from them. This is one thing which I experienced at the Eighth Assembly of the World Council of Churches at Harare in December 1998. In a world under the influence of globalisation, ecumenism itself is also becoming more and more "globalised".

But it seems to me that the most serious reason for a Charta Oecumenica is the challenge of evangelisation. The churches can never be credible in their proclamation of and witness to the Gospel if they show themselves to be disunited and even in conflict with one another. What is at stake is of the essence of the churches and the future of Christianity. One need only think of the urgent need for evangelisation in Asia. I have always been impressed by what John Paul II said at Bucharest at his meeting with Patriarch Teoctist on 8 May 1999, and which he repeated last October: "What can encourage the people of today to believe in Christ, if we continue to tear the seamless garment of the Church... Who will forgive us for this lack of witness?"

Reconciliation among Christians is necessary not only because of the historical situation; it is a demand which is integral to the Gospel itself.

2. The secret of ecumenism

Faced with this urgency and this responsibility, we must go back to the heart of the matter for enlightenment.

I too was in Augsburg on 31 October 1999, when the Lutheran-Catholic Joint Declaration on the Doctrine of Justification was signed. This signing marked an important and irrevocable step towards reconciliation. It signified that the division which took place 500 years ago did not go deep enough to reach the common roots of our faith and keep us from finding our way back to the path of unity. But how did we arrive at this point? Almost 30 years of work gave us a clear indication that we were able to agree as soon as we went back to the Word of God, and when we sought to approach the topics and the problems raised by the Word itself. This has been our guide also in drawing up the Charta Oecumenica. The subtitles of the three chapters each quote a passage from Scripture, and these are the keys to reading the entire text. It is only in the Scriptures that we have been able to find a point of departure which is common to us all. This Word of God reaches its climax, and is fully revealed, in the event of Christ's Passover.

I remember, on Sunday, 29 June 1997, in a large park in the Austrian city of Graz, the closing worship service of the Second European Ecumenical Assembly, which for the space of a week had brought together 10,000 participants from nearly 200 churches, Bishops' Conferences and ecumenical organisations in every country of Europe, and even from other continents. The people around me were celebrating joyfully, but as for me, I was seriously worried about a matter having to do with the organisation for which I was partly responsible. I found that I couldn't celebrate; I even felt disappointed after having worked so hard. I recall precisely the moment when I fixed my eyes on the tall cross which towered over the park, and felt the certainty within me that it would be the Christ who hung crucified on the cross, who cried "My God, my God, why have you forsaken me?" who would bring about unity among Christians, and that those who would have the courage to follow him would be his instruments. At that moment I felt a great peace within me. Chiara Lubich, in her speech at the opening of the Assembly, had said that the secret of reconciliation was found in God the Crucified.

The Charta Oecumenica is the fruit of this European Ecumenical Assembly. It intends first of all to be an instrument through which we can learn from this "ignominious and scandalous" flesh that it is the Crucified God who enters into the wounds of humanity and takes its divisions and sufferings upon himself, all the way to crying out against God's abandonment, all the way to death. It is this God-Man who teaches us the steps we must take to become agents of reconciliation and builders of unity: to have the courage to enter into the divisions, not to observe them from the sidelines; to take the wounds and the divisions upon ourselves and thus to stop them, instead of putting the blame for the conflict on others; to offer a place of welcome, without restrictions or boundaries; to believe in love, to the point of having the courage to give one's life; to know that it is love which brings life to a new beginning.

The first chapter of the Charta says it this way: "Jesus Christ revealed to us on the cross his love and the mystery of reconciliation; as his followers, we intend to do our utmost to overcome the problems and obstacles that still divide the churches."

Sometimes, in the ecumenical movement, there seems to be blockage in certain situations. At such times, it is only if we are able to see in them the presence of the Crucified One, who has already been living in this brokenness and this suffering, that we can glimpse the possibility that all is not lost, that it is still possible to go further.

The source of our confidence that reconciliation among Christians will come is the knowledge that the Crucified is the hidden side of the resurrected Christ, and that living in love as disciples of the Crucified One allows us to share in the life of the resurrected Christ. At the end of the Encounter in Strasbourg, when we signed the Charta, one of the youth delegates said to me: "I can't say what it is exactly, but there is a special feeling here, one can tell that something new has happened." This young person had probably sensed the light and the joy of the Resurrected One among us. Perhaps the most urgent of all ecumenical priorities is this, to allow the Resurrected One to be present among us, by living the Gospel together in mutual love. It is my experience that this presence of Christ is possible in every meeting among Christians of all different confessions, even though we are separated by questions of belief which prevent us, for the time being, from sharing in the Eucharist together. It is he who gives us his light within and among us, making us able to overcome the obstacles we have accumulated in the course of history and to make progress in ecumenical dialogue, and he will guide us towards horizons as yet unknown to us.

3. A star to guide us on our way

There is an Arab proverb which I particularly like: "If you want to plough a straight row, hitch your plough to a star." From my experience, I would say that we are called to orient ourselves by the star par excellence: Jesus, crucified and resurrected. By following in his footsteps we will be travelling on a straight ecumenical path, at this historical moment. Together with all these friends, these brothers and sisters from different churches and communities, over the years I have been able to rediscover and follow some of these footprints of Jesus.

1. We are realising more and more, in the face of what sometimes seem to be insurmountable difficulties, that reconciliation and unity are first of all God's gift. Our hope is not built on our own capabilities, but on Jesus' prayer for unity. That is what guarantees it. A great network of prayer has already been created among all those who join in the prayer of Jesus, that full and visible communion among Christians may be established within history.

2. There is a great current of spirituality being formed today, carrying us to interpret the Gospel through our lives. For me, various obstacles to ecumenism which we are seeing today are not so much theological as cultural, psychological, historical or legalistic, and these are causing our dialogue to "stumble" theologically. Nothing other than living the Gospel can free us from these obstacles and move the theological dialogue forward.

3. Ecumenism is a way of life. We have always insisted that the Charta Oecumenica is not so much another written text as a process. The text is submitted for "critique", but that does not mean intellectual critique, but

24

rather one based on life experience. In September 2002, we had a meeting in Ottmaring, Germany, for delegates from different churches in Europe. We were surprised by the reports from the various countries. The Charta is a living force, even though it lives in different ways. Everywhere it arouses dialogues, encounters, reflections, gestures of reconciliation and shared initiatives.

4. Now the time has come to go deeper. Something new is manifesting itself these days at the ecumenical level: the demand to clarify and to defend the identities of the various churches and communities. This is intended to counter the risk of drifting into relativism, or taking too conciliatory a position, on the basis that real dialogue is only possible if one is aware of one's own identity. Those who are not sufficiently knowledgeable about Christianity or their own church will have nothing to contribute. Nevertheless, this strong demand for identity also conceals the risk of shutting ourselves up in our own fortresses, isolated and self-sufficient. But we need not conduct an ecumenical dialogue which fails to respect the identities of the participants; we must rather develop the dimension of identity and truth to the point where we discover that the gift of the other, our love for one another and our communion partake of the essence of our identities as churches, and of Christian truth. The unity given to us in Jesus Christ does not extinguish our identities, but is rather the only way in which we can fully realise them. We must also deepen our concept of dialogue, until we discover that it is the place where we approach the truth itself, as did the disciples on the road to Emmaus.

5. We are called to broaden our horizons. The Charta is a European text; it is the fruit of work shared among the three great church traditions of Europe, Catholic, Orthodox and Protestant. Its intent is to create a communion above and beyond our national situations, to encourage every local church take responsibility for what happens on our continent, not just in our own country.

6. An ecumenical "people" is coming into being. When we were starting to plan for the European Ecumenical Assembly in Graz, we were imagining a meeting among official delegates from the churches, but increasingly and unexpectedly we are seeing the growth and the self-affirmation of an "ecumenical population".

7. A new ecumenical generation is appearing. It was very significant to see how the young people were actors in the Ecumenical Encounter in

Strasbourg and committed themselves to support the Charta. A new generation is emerging. It is no longer conditioned by our ideologies, and is perhaps more disoriented but freer and more ready to appropriate the Gospel for itself. Our part is to entrust to this generation the ecumenical witness.

The road ahead is long - the Charta Oecumenica being the first document of its kind in history - but it is good to put it to work together. We do not yet know where our final destination will be, but God knows.

How the Charta Oecumenica Came to Be

Viorel Ionita

"The ecumenical fellowship is currently in a difficult situation as a result of various factors. This requires conscious counter-strategies. It seems necessary to foster an ecumenical culture of living and working together, and to create a firm basis for it." Having made this observation, the Second European Ecumenical Assembly (EEA2, Graz, Austria, 23-29 June 1997) recommended that the churches throughout Europe "develop a common study document containing basic ecumenical duties and rights. From this a series of ecumenical guidelines, rules and criteria could be developed which would help the churches, those in positions of responsibility and all members, to distinguish between proselytism and Christian witness, as well as between fundamentalism and genuine faithfulness, and help to shape the relationships between majority and minority churches in an ecumenical spirit." (See Reconciliation - gift of God and source of new life, Documents from the Second European Ecumenical Assembly in Graz, published by CCEE and CEC, edited by Rüdiger Noll and Stefan Vesper, Verlag Styria 1998, p. 49)

This recommendation assumed that the European churches need a clear and concrete basis for their ecumenical work together, and also some rules for their conduct towards one another, especially in case of controversies or even conflicts. At a consultation to evaluate the EEA2, organised jointly by the Conference of European Churches (CEC) and the Evangelical Academy at Loccum, Germany, 18-20 October 1997, it was observed that the experience of the Assembly in Graz showed that "the churches in Europe need to develop a new common language, in order to create a firm basis for their ecumenical relations and an ecumenical culture of living and praying together."

In view of today's new ecumenical tasks and challenges, the European churches needed a new instrument, that is, an ecumenical charter, so that they could enter into new paths together. At a consultation held by the Council of European Bishops' Conferences (CCEE) in Prague, 30 January - 1 February 1998, it was emphasised that the ecumenical charter should foster cooperation amongst European churches in view of "common support for projects on behalf of humanity, and of building a new Europe."

At its Assembly in October 1997, CCEE decided to join together with CEC in the initiative of drawing up a Charta Oecumenica in the light of the recommendation from Graz. Similarly, at the first meeting of the CEC Central Committee elected at the 11th Assembly in Graz, it was decided to join together with CCEE in working towards a Charta Oecumenica for Europe.

Subsequently the CCEE/CEC Joint Committee, at its meeting in Rome (Vatican City, 19-22 February 1998), recommended that the two organisations "begin working together towards a Charta Oecumenica". The recommendations of the Joint Committee in Rome were, among others, that the Charta should have the following character and content:
- "a relatively brief text",
- "which is neither dogma, nor ecclesiastical law, nor an international political statement",
- "based on the Holy Scriptures and referring to previous ecumenical statements, such as the WCC's Costly Unity and the Roman Catholic Church's Directorium",
- "containing principles and criteria for promoting ecumenical commitment among the churches in Europe",
- "and which promotes a learning process towards an 'ecumenical culture' and a 'culture of dialogue' among the churches in Europe".

For CEC and CCEE it was important from the beginning of this project that it would not produce a text which would be put away in the drawers of church offices, like so many other ecumenical texts, but rather would lead to a complex process of discussion, in which the European churches, the Bishops' Conferences, the Associated Organisations of CEC and CCEE, and groups and individuals within the churches would participate actively.

As a first step in this task, the Joint Committee recommended the formation of a Working Group composed of eight members in all, which was to prepare a first draft of the Charta. Members named by CCEE to this Working Group were Don Aldo Giordano, General Secretary; P. Remi Hoeckman, OP; Prof. Dr. Ilona Riedel-Sprangenberger and Prof. Dr.

Waclaw Hryniewicz. Members named by CEC included Dr. Keith Clements, General Secretary; Prof. Reinhard Frieling, Evangelical Church in Germany, Rev. Giovanna Sciclone, Waldensian Church of Italy, Fr. Vladimir Schmaly, Russian Orthodox Church and Prof. Dr. Grigorios Larentzakis, Ecumenical Patriarchate. This Working Group met at the Centre de Rencontres in Cartigny, near Geneva, from 22 to 24 October 1998, where, after a thorough and constructive discussion, it made the following recommendations for a Charta Oecumenica:

"With regard to content:

1) The Charta Oecumenica should be a brief, positive and encouraging document.

2) The Charta is to be adopted by the churches, to be for the churches and has to do with relations among Christians.

3) The ecumenical character of the Charta should be emphasised.

4) It should also be a European Charta, for the Europe of today.

5) It is not to be an appeal, nor a political statement, nor a working paper. It should be a theological text, but not a theological tract.

6) The churches should be involved in drawing up the Charta.

7) This Charta, as well as the process of drawing it up, should contribute to an ecumenical culture and a culture of dialogue".

"With regard to form:

1) Part One: indicative - confessing our common faith; no alternative to ecumenism; using expressions from the Bible as far as possible

2) Part Two: imperative - the churches and Christians of Europe commit themselves to live in ecumenical fellowship

3) Part Three: concrete implications for relations between majority and minority churches, for proselytism, for differences in approach to ethical questions; how do we deal with history; structures for dialogue between churches."

This first draft was thoroughly discussed at the CCEE/CEC Joint Committee meeting in Guernsey, UK, 4-7 March 1999. The Joint Committee made the following recommendations with regard to the draft:

- "that the final text of the Charta not be longer than the present draft version";

- "that the draft version be submitted only once to the churches and Bishops' Conferences for their responses, namely in summer (1999)".

- "At its meeting at the beginning of the year 2001, the CEC/CCEE Joint Committee will adopt the final version".

- "In a ceremony during the CEC/CCEE Ecumenical Encounter in 2001, the final text of the Charta Oecumenica will be signed by the two Presidents of CEC and CCEE, calling upon the European churches and Bishops' Conferences to make this Charta their own."

As a further step towards a European Charta Oecumenica, the Joint Committee proposed that a consultation be held, with about 50 participants representing some of the CEC member churches and some of the European Bishops' Conferences. At this consultation, the Cartigny draft was to be discussed in detail by a larger group.

This consultation was held in Graz, Austria, 30 April - 3 May 1999. The agenda included two papers on the question of a European Charta Oecumenica. The first, by Prof. Waclaw Hryniewicz of CCEE, from Poland, was entitled "Ecumenism and Its Difficulties Today: theological considerations especially with regard to the situation in Eastern Europe". The second speaker, representing CEC, was Dr. Fritz Erich Anhelm from Germany, with a paper entitled "A Charta Oecumenica for the European Churches".

In a general discussion on the first draft of the Charta, it was remarked that this Charta should not only stimulate further ecumenical cooperation amongst European churches, but should also represent a way of receiving the results of previous ecumenical conversations.

The draft of the Charta, after being revised in the light of the discussion at the consultation in Graz, was sent in July 1999 to the CEC member churches, the Bishops' Conferences and the Associated Organisations of CCEE and CEC, asking them to discuss it thoroughly within their own contexts. In the accompanying letter, signed by the Presidents of CCEE and CEC, the churches and Bishops' Conferences were requested to send their responses by 1 September 2000 to either CCEE or CEC.

The CEC/CCEE Joint Committee discussed the Charta Oecumenica process in detail at its meeting in Prague (3-6 February 2000), and also stated that it regarded the current draft as basically good. The Joint Committee recommended that in the further process the Charta should not be completely rewritten, "but should retain its particular characteristics. It is open to changes, but should not become packed with too much material and too long."

In support of the Charta process, General Secretary Keith Clements wrote to the CEC member churches on 20 March 2000, to encourage them in their discussions of the Charta Oecumenica and to remind them to send their responses by 1st September. The General Secretary emphasised further that: "... even at this interim stage, if you have not already done so it would be of great help and interest if you could let me know how the response is being conducted in your own church or organisation, or of any special events and activities (consultations, publications etc). Equally, we would be grateful to know of any particular problems being encountered in initiating such work. In this way, we can gain as complete a picture as possible on how the Charta is being dealt with right across Europe."

At the suggestion of both sponsoring organisations, the draft of the Charta was translated into at least 16 other European languages, besides the official languages of German (the original), English and French, and was very widely distributed.

National councils of churches and ecumenical working groups also made known their interest in taking part in this process.

By 30 September 2000, the CEC secretariat in Geneva had received 75 responses to the draft of the Charta Oecumenica, from member churches, various Associated Organisations of CEC, various churches or ecumenical organisations not formally connected with CEC, and from individuals.

On the CCEE side, by 29 September the St. Gallen office had received 20 responses and papers from Bishops' Conferences as well as some 50 responses from various Catholic organisations and groups.

CCEE remarked that "the responses in general gave evidence of serious work in depth. They are very interesting in the understanding they provide of the relationships among the various churches and church fellowships in Europe, and about the meeting-points in the ecumenical movement today." All the Bishops' Conferences welcomed the project and sought to encourage it as a means of waking up the ecumenical process which seemed to have fallen asleep lately. Some said it would be useful in work with local churches, others found it important at European level. Some Conferences said that the draft of the Charta was already proving very important at the local level, since it offered an opportunity for relations among Christians to grow.

The responses from churches, ecumenical organisations and groups and from individuals differed widely from one another, but all showed what serious discussion of the Charta Oecumenica had taken place. Many churches and organisations explained in their covering letters, or in the introductions to their papers, how they had worked with the Charta. For example, some had published their responses on their Websites. The responses also differed in their structure.

Some critical comments by various churches and ecumenical groups began with the title. Some churches wondered why an expression in Latin was chosen, the usefulness of which depends on who will use the document. Other churches had trouble with this title as such, and proposed others. The Russian Orthodox Church suggested using only the subtitle: For co-operation among the churches in Europe. The Ecumenical Council in Denmark suggested as subtitle, Guidelines for cooperation among the churches in Europe.

Many responses show that the churches were not clear about who the addressees of the Charta should be. The use of "we", which includes everyone and no one, was said not to be suitable for a statement of commitment.

The statements of commitment, for many of those who responded, were too general and did not go far enough. For others, the statements of commitment were too strong and should at the most be formulated as recommendations. Several churches even expected, perhaps in an appendix, some thoughts, at least, on setting up checking mechanisms to see whether the parties keep the commitments they have made. Most of these commitments seemed to be so formulated as to make it impossible from the start to check whether they are being implemented.

There were some comments that the tone of the Charta is very modest, while others thought it "needs to be more modest". The purpose of the Charta Oecumenica should be considered in connection with the Charter of Basic Human Rights. For others the tone of the Charta was too "church-centred".

Various western European churches find the language of the present draft of the Charta to be very much "coloured" by the context of the Orthodox majority countries. But the same text impressed some central and eastern European churches as too "western", or they felt that this draft is based on a too "liberal Protestant" understanding of the church. Other churches, furthermore, had the impression that the draft is too much influenced by Orthodox-

Catholic issues, and that the concerns of minority churches, such as Pentecostal and emigrant churches, are given hardly any consideration, or none at all. On the other hand it was said that there was no mention of the fundamentally different approaches of western and eastern churches.

With regard to the content of the Charta, on which almost all responses had comments and proposals for change, the following issues definitely needed further clarification, even in the absence of unanimity on them:
- Eucharist and intercelebration
- distinguishing between a church and a sect
- proselytism
- concept of the unity of the church; use of the confession of faith of 381
- the one baptism
- the concept "to profess" (faith or loyalty) with regard to Europe
- ecumenical spirituality
- mission and evangelisation
- dialogue with other religions

All the responses were by and large in agreement with the third part of the Charta, which speaks of the common responsibility of the churches towards Europe, although there were many questions and suggestions for changes to it. It was said that this is the most important part of the Charta, and that this part could be the basis for the entire document. One church would like to see this part more in the context of the entire world. Another response said that the formulations on Europe (text referring to the EU) are open to misapprehension and must be totally removed, and it must be clearly defined what is meant by Europe.

Some responses suggest that the issue of relations with the people Israel (Judaism in the text) be dealt with in a separate paragraph on relations with other religions; a paragraph 10 is proposed. One response, however, expresses the opinion that the use of the term "chosen people" amounts to unequal treatment of the other religions, and therefore the accent on relations with Muslims and with Jews is unacceptable.

The Drafting Committee studied all the responses carefully and gave them consideration in drawing up a final version of the Charta Oecumenica text. As a first step, after a general discussion about the various responses from the churches and Bishops' Conferences, the Committee began by working in three separate confessional groups: a Catholic, an Orthodox and a Protestant group. When they came back together, the groups shared their concerns about some points they wanted to emphasise, and the way in which these emphases should be taken into account in the new version of the Charta.

From the Orthodox viewpoint, the following points were set forth:
a) the draft proposal from the meeting of the Orthodox representatives in Crete (2000) is supported by the churches which were represented there;
b) the confession of faith of 381 should be mentioned;
c) the new draft should not contain any ecclesiological statements;
d) the reference to forced conversion to a different faith (point 4.29) should be retained;
e) the issue of European unity and its Christian values should be clarified further, making sure it is plain that churches and not politicians are speaking here.

From the Catholic viewpoint, the following points were recommended for closer examination:

a) as questions regarding the document from the Orthodox representatives in Crete:
- why was the reference to common prayer taken out?
- why was the term ecumenical movement questioned?
- why was the section on mission and evangelisation shortened?
b) more consideration should be given to the one baptism;
c) the attitude toward the people Israel;
d) Christian values and Europe:
- Europe and the poor;
- Europe may not be reduced to the European Union alone;
e) the concept of sects should either be defined more precisely, or left out;
f) whether the title Charta Oecumenica should continue to be used;
g) there should be no inflation of the commitments;
h) how should the Charta process be continued? For CCEE it seems possible at this point that the Charta could be signed in Strasbourg.

The small Protestant group offered the following points for further consideration:
a) how should the reference to the confession of faith of 381 be formulated in the Charta?
b) common mission and evangelisation should be underlined;

c) religious freedom should be clearly affirmed;

d) what about the concept of sects?

e) how are we seeing the communication among the churches here?

f) what is the understanding of church unity here? the search for eucharistic fellowship should be emphasised;

g) interreligious dialogue;

h) Europe: the churches must not be misused for separation within Europe. We should not use the expression "a soul for Europe".

i) the minority churches should receive more consideration;

j) ecumenical spirituality: the issue of diversity in spirituality;

After a detailed discussion on the responses from the churches and Bishops' Conferences throughout Europe, the Drafting Committee prepared a second draft, which was then submitted to the Joint Committee.

After the Drafting Committee meeting, CCEE and CEC published a joint press communique, in which they said: "At the European Ecumenical Encounter in Strasbourg, in Easter week 2001, the draft of the Charta will play an important role. The Charta Oecumenica process, its reception and its implementation will accompany the churches in Europe for a number of years to come. This is a clear sign of a firm determination to seek new paths to dialogue and reconciliation."

At its meeting in Porto, Portugal, 26-29 January 2001, the CEC/CCEE Joint Committee discussed the second draft of the Charta and declared it to be a Basis Text which should be signed at the European Ecumenical Encounter in Strasbourg (EEE2001).

The Charta Oecumenica was presented at the youth preparatory meeting for the EEE2001 in Strasbourg and amply discussed. The discussion had to do not with editing the text, but rather how the Charta can be received and put into practice in the European churches. As a result of these discussions, in a statement at the end of the closing worship service on Sunday, 22 April, the youth delegates committed themselves to continue to carry the Charta Oecumenica forward in their respective contexts and to put it into practice. In an Encounter plenary session, one of the youth delegates stated that "young people are not so concerned about the doctrinal aspect of the statement. The text must show that we intend to travel together; the document must be continued in real life."

During the EEE2001 itself, the Charta was introduced on Friday afternoon in a meeting at the Council of Europe, 20 April, by Professors Ilona Riedel-Spangenberger, Reinhard Frieling, Grigorios Larentzakis and Father Christian Foster. The newspaper Dernières Nouvelles d'Alsace, in its report on the Encounter on 21 April, wrote that "At the Council of Europe, youth and their elders bore witness to their personal Christian pilgrimages."

On Saturday, 21 April the Charta was discussed in four working groups. In one of these groups it was remarked that "The Charta is a station at which to stop and refuel, a place with fresh water, a place to regain strength. Tomorrow we will arrive at this station. On leaving this station, let us continue our ecumenical journey with fresh courage and with a new dynamic." . On the working group discussions, the newspaper Rheinischer Merkur of 20 April 2001 reported: "Seldom has an ecumenical discussion paper received such a wide response as has the Charta Oecumenica."

The signing of the Charta Oecumenica by the CEC and CCEE Presidents, Metropolitan Jérémie and Cardinal Vlk, on Sunday, 22 April, was seen by many of those present as the high point of the Encounter. With the signing of the Charta in Strasbourg, the second and most important phase in the Charta process has begun. Since then it has become the task of the churches and the Bishops' Conferences throughout Europe to continue working with the Charta, to make it their own.

After all the church representatives of the churches and youth organisations who were present in Strasbourg had taken the Charta home with them in backpacks, the Charta was officially sent to all the churches and Bishops' Conferences with an accompanying letter from the CEC and CCEE General Secretaries. In their letter of 30 April 2001, Don Aldo Giordano and the Revd. Dr. Keith Clements said it was a joy for them, "to transmit officially to you the final text of the Charta Oecumenica - Guidelines for the Growing Cooperation among the Churches in Europe."

After a summary description of the Encounter in Strasbourg and of the process of drafting the Charta Oecumenica, the General Secretaries made the following comment: "It is also important to bear in mind the status of the Charta, and we therefore request that the Preamble be read carefully. As it has no magisterial or dogmatic character, nor is it legally binding under church law, the text does not directly deal with ecclesiological issues, and uses the term 'church' as it is understood from each of the subjects involved in the initiative. Furthermore, it will be seen that in the protocol attached to the document and signed by the Presidents of CEC and CCEE, the Charta is commended to the churches as a Basis Text offered to them by CEC and CCEE. As such it is not intended for further revision. But it is hoped that the churches and ecumenical bodies in Europe will receive, study and further discuss the Charta and take concrete steps towards its implementation, if necessary building upon it and adapting it according to their local and national contexts."

Since April 2001 the Charta Oecumenica is with all the churches and Bishops' Conferences, which are now endeavouring to make this Charta their own concern, in the hope that its acceptance and implementation will lead the ecumenical movement in Europe along new paths.

The Signing of the Charta Oecumenica - Strasbourg 2001

Viorel Ionita and Sarah Numico

The European Ecumenical Encounter 2001 (EEE2001) was convened at the request of the Council of European Bishops' Conferences (CCEE) and the Conference of European Churches (CEC), that the churches might reflect together, at the beginning of the third Christian millennium, about the meaning of faith in Jesus Christ for today's world. The Encounter was purposefully held in 2001 instead of 2000, because in 2001 all the churches in the world celebrated Easter on the same Sunday, 15 April. The EEE2001 did not take place during Easter itself, but was held early in the Easter season as observed by all churches, from Thursday, 19 April to Sunday afternoon 22 April 2001, in Strasbourg, France.

I. The Strasbourg meeting brought together, in the first place, the members of the CCEE Assembly with the members of the CEC Central Committee. Furthermore, it was an encounter between these two groups on one hand and about a hundred youth delegates from almost all the churches and Christian youth organisations in Europe on the other. CCEE and CEC each invited an additional 15 church leaders to participate in the encounter with the young people.

CEC and CCEE hoped that this would be a real encounter, with sharing and dialogue not only among confessions but also between generations, in the effort to promote a vision for the future of the Christian faith in Europe. It was also to be a contribution towards fulfilling a commitment made at the Second European Ecumenical Assembly in 1997 in Graz, "to involve young people, entrusting to them the ecumenical vision for the future, and also to take forward the conciliar process concerning justice, peace and the integrity of creation".

About a hundred youth delegates arrived in Strasbourg in the afternoon of 17 April and were all lodged together at a youth centre. Their preparatory meeting gave the young people a chance to get to know one another and to prepare together for their encounter with the older church leaders. The meeting included a number of workshops on various concerns which are dealt with in the Charta Oecumenica, and also on the question of what should be done next with the Charta.

One of the youth delegates summed up this experience by saying that there had been "various high points during these days, with the whole group and for each of us personally - in plenary sessions, in worship, during free time. Besides having so many valuable insights and ideas to take with us, the best of all was having a lasting impression that, as John Paul II said, 'The ecumenical way is irrevocable' - it is our way."

A number of the young people thanked the older church leaders for the attitude of great simplicity with which they accepted the dialogue and the encounter. As they were leaving, many of the youth also promised to be in the forefront of distributing the Charta Oecumenica and implementing it at the local level.

The older CEC and CCEE delegates arrived in Strasbourg on Wednesday, 18 April, and were assigned together to another lodging than that in which the youth were housed. From 15h00 on Wednesday to Thursday afternoon, CEC and CCEE held their own separate meetings at the Palais Universitaire. The CCEE Assembly elected as its new President Bishop Amédée Grab from Chur, Switzerland. In the evening of the same day CCEE held its 30th anniversary celebration, to which CEC was invited.

II. The opening ceremony of the EEE2001 took place on Thursday, 19 April, at 16h00 in the main auditorium (Aula) of Strasbourg University. Following the opening speeches by CEC President Metropolitan Jérémie and outgoing CCEE President Cardinal Vlk, there was a series of welcoming speeches from the local authorities. Messages were also read from, among others, the Ecumenical Patriarch Bartholomaios I and Patriarch Alexy II of Moscow and all Russia. The message from Pope John Paul II emphasised that "a clear proclamation of the Gospel is especially urgently needed in Europe."

As an introduction to the Encounter theme, and especially as a example of discussion between youth and older church leaders, this first session also included a dialogue between Pastor Elfriede Dörr and Cardinal Karl Lehmann about their expectations of the Encounter. Thus, on one hand the youth were encouraged to engage in dialogue with the older church representatives, and on the other the older representatives were motivated to be open to dialogue with the youth representatives.

The EEE2001 opening worship service was held on Thursday, 19 April at 18h30 in the Catholic Cathedral of Strasbourg. Besides the participants in the Encounter, a large number of church members from Strasbourg and its environs attended the service. Archbishop Joseph Pierre Doré of Strasbourg welcomed all present in the name of the host church. The sermon on Matthew 28.1-10 was preached by the Revd. Dr. Elisabeth Parmentier of the Church of the Augsburg Confession of Alsace and Lorraine, who offered Christian guidance for the Encounter, and indeed for all Christians, as follows: "We come from that Easter morning when he arose who, by his cross, had broken down the wall of hate between human beings. And we are going to meet him who promised that from now on he would never leave us, but always be in our midst. We are moving towards our centre, whatever are the roundabout human routes we take to get there. Our Galilee is our permanent re-orientation towards the Christ who is in our midst."

III. The entire Encounter programme was held within the framework of the morning and evening worship services, which took place in the Reformed St. Paul's Church near the university, as follows:
- Common morning prayers according to the Protestant tradition, Friday, 20 April
- Common evening prayers according to the Catholic tradition, Friday, 20 April
- Ecumenical service of morning prayer, Saturday, 21 April
- Common evening prayers according to the Orthodox tradition, Saturday, 21 April

The preachers at these various services were Bishop Finn Wagle, Church of Norway; Bishop Virgil Bercea, Greek Catholic Church in Romania; and the Very Revd. John Arnold, Church of England. In his meditation, Bishop Wagle characterised the Encounter as a fellowship of travellers: "We have found one another, Christians from different denominations in Europe, a Europe where Christians and their churches haven't always looked upon the Christian life as companionship on the journey, sometimes almost the opposite. We have found one another in travelling together along the road of faith. And now we want to travel on - together."

On Sunday morning, 22 April, there were first worship services according to four Christian confessions in four different churches in

Strasbourg. Then the participants came as pilgrims from four directions to the Protestant St. Thomas Church, where the closing worship service was held. Besides the 250 or so Encounter participants, this service was attended by many people from the city and surrounding area, and even from Germany and Switzerland.

This service was led by the Revd. OKRin Rut Rohrandt (EKD) and Cardinal Roger Etchegaray (Vatican). The congregation was welcomed by Prof. Marc Lienhard, Moderator of the Church of the Augsburg Confession of Alsace and Lorraine. The sermon, on Matthew 28.20, was preached by Archbishop Anastasios of Tirana and All Albania (Orthodox Church), who closed his sermon with the following words: "Proceed with the certainty that 'all things' are under the power of the resurrected Lord, not only all humanity, but even the entire creation. Instead of an economic globalisation which leads to the exploitation of many, let us struggle, each according to his or her abilities and opportunities, toward an ecumenical brotherhood that rests upon freedom, respect for one another, and love, which emanate from the cross and the life-giving tomb of the resurrected Christ."

Following the closing worship service, representatives of the youth delegates read a message in which they committed themselves to support and to spread the Charta Oecumenica, each in his or her own context. The General Secretaries of CCEE and CEC, Don Aldo Giordano and the Revd. Dr. Keith Clements, thanked all who had worked and participated in the Encounter. Then followed the ceremony of signing of the Charta Oecumenica by the CEC and CCEE Presidents. Cardinal Vlk read a passage from the Bible, and Metropolitan Jérémie offered a beautiful prayer of sending forth.

Each of these moments of shared prayer, as well as the signing of the Charta Oecumenica, was regarded by many of those present an important part of the Encounter. The same was true of the Bible studies on Friday and Saturday mornings. On the first day, following morning prayers at St. Paul's, each participant had received a card with a picture of Jesus with the two disciples on the road to Emmaus. On the back of the card were questions to stimulate sharing about how each participant had celebrated Easter. The participants were then sent out in pairs, each consisting of a youth delegate and an older church leader. Overall this Emmaus experience was very well received, and many found it an extraordinary experience.

The Saturday morning Bible study was led by Cardinal Cormac Murphy O'Connor and Bishop Bärbel Wartenberg-Potter. "Paul writes us a poem about the power of faith, hope and love," said Bishop Wartenberg Potter in her study on 1 Cor. 13.13. "One of the many characteristics of love is the one we especially need in conversations, in the way we treat each other: the macrothymia, the big-heartedness, easygoingness, staying power and dogged patience, the wind of the long distance runner. Without it we will never find the way to one another."

IV. The main theme of the EEE2001, "I am with you always, to the end of the world", was developed through the following sub-themes:

Friday: Who are you for me? In the light of the disciples' experience on the road to Emmaus, we shared with one another the meaning of Christ for our personal lives and for our churches.

Saturday: Where are you leading us? We asked one another how we live in faith, hope and love.

Sunday: Where are you sending us? As each of us received a backpack containing a copy of the Charta Oecumenica, we helped one another to become aware of our mission and responsibility for proclaiming the Gospel, and for the life of women and men in Europe and throughout the entire planet.

As an introduction to the main theme, Metropolitan Daniel (Orthodox Patriarchate of Romania) gave a paper entitled "Jesus Christ - Image of the unseen God revealed through the Holy Spirit". Following his statement of the theological basis for the theme, the Metropolitan invited the churches of Europe to "today confess Christ crucified, resurrected and glorified: the victory of holiness over sin, the victory of love over hate, the victory of peace over violence, the victory of justice over injustice, the victory of light over darkness, so that the world may receive joy from the kingdom of God."

The plenary session was then divided into groups of eight persons each, including youth and older church leaders at each table. This gave everyone the opportunity to share personal experiences and encounters with the resurrected Lord. Rev. Rut Rohrandt and the Roman Catholic priest Paul Hüster of the German (Roman Catholic) Bishops' Conference introduced and supported this process.

On Friday afternoon, 20 April, two sessions were held in the plenary hall of the Council of Europe. There the EEE2001 participants were welcomed by Bruno Haller, General Secretary of the Council of Europe Parliamentary Assembly. In his speech he said that with the Charta Oecumenica the churches had set an example for the politicians.

The participants said later that the time of personal testimonies which followed was one of the impressions which remained with them the most strongly. Persons from different backgrounds - youth, older church leaders, and politicians - spoke of the power and beauty of their own experiences of Jesus Christ: Cardinal Roger Etchegaray, Roman Catholic; the Very Revd. Margarethe Isberg, Protestant; Dr. Michael Weninger, European Union, Roman Catholic; Ms. Julia Kokoshari, Syndesmos delegate, Orthodox; Mr. Vlad Naumescu, Greek Catholic from Romania; the Revd. John Murray, Council of Europe, Anglican; and Brother Luke of Taizé. A close relationship could be noted between personal experience of the Gospel and a commitment to working within history and politics.

There is a public dimension to Christianity, which calls for involvement in the world. It was important for the churches to make a common witness to the European institutions. A journalist commented on this moment as follows: "Many different testimonies, many different objects as symbols - but the same Christ. It is hard to say what weight the afternoon of 20 April 2001 at the Council of Europe will carry in ecumenical history. But to say that at the end the faces of all those present were radiant, without exception, does not require rhetoric."

In the second session at the Council of Europe, discussion of the Charta Oecumenica was introduced by Professors Ilona Riedel-Spangenberger, Reinhard Frieling and Grigorios Larentzakis, and by Father Christian Foster. The first three had made decisive contributions as members of the drafting committee for the Charta. This presentation on the Charta served to introduce the discussion in the four working groups which met the next morning at the University. The four speakers acted as moderators for these groups.

One of these groups said in reporting on its work that "the Charta should be the sign of a new beginning. It should stimulate a culture of dialogue, a long-term encounter characterised by openness, honesty and trust. The 'ecumenical culture' must be the culture of such an open and fair dialogue. Then the Charta will have authority. It will have authority and the force of an obligation if it promotes the ecumenical culture of dialogue in countries, in churches, in Bishops' Conferences, in dioceses and parishes, and in the different situations in which Christians in Europe live. We were agreed that, as the title of the first section expresses it, we are all 'called together to unity in faith'."

One of the young people said of the Charta Oecumenica, "It is really in the hearts of us young people. We have been looking forward to its signing, hoping that this word would 'become flesh'... for us as youth, ecumenical dialogue has absolute priority."

On Saturday afternoon there were first separate meetings of the youth on the one hand and the older CEC and CCEE representatives on the other, in which the participants were to ask whether their expectations of this Encounter had been fulfilled. There then followed the final plenary session of the EEE2001, in which another dialogue was held between Rev. Elfriede Dörr and Cardinal Karl Lehmann. This time the topic was what participants could take home with them from this Encounter.

The participants in the EEE2001 had had various opportunities for informal conversation with one another, at working groups and work-shops, on the way from their lodgings to the university or to church, and also on a boat trip through the canals of the city of Strasbourg. After the closing worship service and the signing of the Charta Oecumenica in St. Thomas' Church, both youth and older delegates felt like members of the one ecumenical family in Europe.

In her evaluation during her dialogue with Cardinal Lehmann at the final session, the young pastor, Elfriede Dörr, said: "The concept of ecumenism, which was our concern here in Strasbourg, had its day in the form of 'ecumenical encounter'. This meeting had plenty of space for encounters. It was conceived and planned so as to offer possibilities for young and old, men and women, church leaders and youth to encounter one another. There was real listening and speaking, questioning and enquiring, getting to know one another and opening ourselves to being known."

V. The Encounter in Strasbourg received a great deal of attention from the press in various countries, especially in Germany, France, Italy and Switzerland. Besides the church press, there were also articles in such newspapers as the Frankfurter Allgemeine, Süddeutsche Zeitung, General-Anzeiger and Le Monde, to name a few of the best-known. There were some critical comments in evaluating the way the EEE2001 was conducted, especially from those who had expected strong disagreements or something more spectacular, but overall this Encounter was assessed positively by the press.

At a meeting of the CEC and CCEE General Secretaries on 21-22 May in Arbon, Switzerland, it was judged that the aims of the EEE2001 had been fulfilled. Some negative aspects were also mentioned: during the preparations it had not been easy to find a balance between the needs of the youth and those of the older church leaders. To the last, the purpose of the Charta Oecumenica was not clear to everyone. The level of the delegations sent by some churches did not meet expectations. Some of the young people wanted to see more visibility and a more important role for the youth. Strasbourg was a very meaningful venue at symbolic and aesthetic levels, but had created many logistical difficulties and especially did not offer lodgings where all participants could be together.

Nevertheless, the Encounter in Strasbourg was a clear success. It was the fruit of the efforts, prayers and unity of a great many people, and has the value of the fellowship that was experienced there. It is hard to say what contribution the Encounter in Strasbourg has made to the ecumenical movement in Europe, but a few elements may be noted:

- The newness of youth participation. Young people speak explicitly and fearlessly about their faith experiences and look for credible witnesses. Their need for transparency and a good example is good for older people. The elders, for their part, can help the younger people not to stop with their own personal experiences, but to enter into the great tradition of the church and become aware of the weight of differences among the confessions.

- That place was given to worshipping together, but according to the different traditions, was not experienced as a step backward. These worship services helped participants to understand that reconciliation does not have to deprive us of the riches of our different traditions.

- The Charta Oecumenica represents an opportunity which we now have in Europe.

- On various occasions it became evident that a little humour makes an important contribution to the ecumenical movement. It might have been useful to make fun of ourselves a little, to avoid putting ourselves at centre stage, to stop seeking attention for ourselves, but instead to turn our attention to Christ, our only Saviour.

- At the end of the Encounter, the joy of what people had experienced was palpable. One said, "I can't say what it is exactly, but there is a clear feeling that something new has happened. Perhaps it is that, like the disciples on the road to Emmaus, we have experienced the light and the joy of Jesus."

II. READING THE CHARTA OECUMENICA FROM A THEOLOGICAL PERSPECTIVE

We Believe in "One Holy Catholic and Apostolic Church"

Grigorios Larentzakis

It is always a joy when new, concrete steps are taken in the ecumenical movement towards realising the longed-for communion among the churches.

Two high points for ecumenical cooperation at the all-European level, very stimulating for building a new Europe, have been the first European Ecumenical Assembly in Basel, in May 1989, on the theme "Peace with Justice", and the Second European Ecumenical Assembly in Graz, 23-29 June 1997, on the theme "Reconciliation - Gift of God, Source of New Life". Both were jointly organised by the Conference of European Churches and the Council of (Roman Catholic) Bishops' Conferences in Europe. All the documents from these two European assemblies are very important and worth reading, but we also have a further noteworthy consequence from them. In the spirit of these two European Ecumenical Assemblies, on a recommendation from Graz, the Charta Oecumenica has been created.

When the Presidents of both organisations placed their signatures at the end of this document, commending it to the churches, a week after the common celebration of the greatest Christian festival, that of Christ's Resurrection, a very serious ecumenical event took place. These two main church/ecumenical organisations in Europe have found their way to an intensively shared ecumenical journey. Now they were making known the intention of all Europe's churches to support this journey towards koinonia among the churches, to follow it themselves and to quicken its pace as they are able. We already have a lot of ecumenical documents, and those who say we have far too many may not be entirely wrong. But the character of this one, the Charta Oecumenica, has been significantly different from the beginning, thus living up to the intention of the 1997 Second European Ecumenical Assembly in Graz.

The steps leading to the Charta Oecumenica were logical and consistent. We are always hearing it said, and even deplored, that we only move forward step by step, and some even say these are always only "first steps"; but the Charta Oecumenica represents one of the most important ecumenical steps. This document is more like the platform and foundation upon which we can safely take steps, always assuming that we are serious about restoring the unity of the churches.

The Charta Oecumenica is the first document that belongs to all the Christian churches in Europe, containing "Guidelines for the Growing Cooperation among the Churches in Europe". I would propose that it be used not only in church circles, but also when working with other institutions and with politicians, for I am convinced that it contains important and indispensable principles and indications also for political decision-making in Europe, today and tomorrow. Not only because this Charta Oecumenica continually emphasises the dignity of every human person, created in God's image, as the basis of human society, not only because the Charta stands up against all discrimination, marginalisation and exclusive nationalism, not only because it calls for reconciliation among all peoples, but because it also articulates "Our Common Responsibility in Europe" very clearly and unmistakably. The Charta Oecumenica also does not ignore the existence of the other religions in Europe, such as Judaism and Islam, but rather recommends that a way of dialogue be sought together with them, and of working together on common problems. It also promotes everyone's own initiative. It is a solid basic text for further concrete work.

These are some basic observations. I now turn to the Preamble and Part I. After praise and thanks to the Triune God for the fellowship that has grown up among us, the churches' resolve is clearly expressed to repent and to work "to overcome the divisions still existing among us". The Charta Oecumenica unambiguously recognises that we still have divisions which must be overcome. We should not, as many people do, regard the existence of separate confessional churches which not infrequently compete with one another, even though they may no longer be fighting openly, as a blessing or a gift of God. The Charta Oecumenica is very realistic, aware that if we do not overcome these divisions we cannot "credibly proclaim the message of the Gospel among all people". This is what it is about: the credibility and efficacy of the church itself.

Here I would also like to emphasise that the Charta Oecumenica sets out, beginning in its introduction, an unmistakable definition of Europe which must be respected. Our European continent reaches "from the Atlantic to the Urals, from the North Cape to the Mediterranean". So it means all of Europe and not just central and/or western Europe, with which "Europe" is often identified. This definition of Europe in the Charta Oecumenica was not settled upon by chance, but after mature reflection and very purposefully. In this whole of Europe live all its peoples, each with its own characteristic identity, and all together they make up our continent's diverse structure, whether they are EU members or not, or not yet. I would wish that when politicians are talking about or conducting negotiations with new EU candidates, they would avoid using expressions which may offend the dignity of these people, such as whether or not they are "ready" or "ripe" for Europe. What does it take to be "ready" or "ripe"? We may also hear that some people are not ready to "come into" Europe, or that the boundary of Europe is moving eastward. Is the European Union identical with Europe?

What is the character of the Charta Oecumenica? It contains guidelines, but also commitments. Does it have the character of commitment in a dogmatic sense, or as under church law? One thing is clear: neither the Conference of European Churches alone, nor it together with the (Catholic) Council of Bishops' Conferences, constitutes a "super-church" which can give instructions to the member churches. Nor, as we well know, is the World Council of Churches such a super-church. Thus the Charta Oecumenica states clearly and unmistakably, so that no church need misunderstand or be afraid, that "it has no magisterial or dogmatic character, nor is it legally binding under church law". This has caused some to say that, with this explanation, the Charta has relativised itself and damaged its own efficacy. We must hope that the content of this entire paragraph of the preamble will be taken very seriously for the meaning of the Charta Oecumenica: "In this spirit, we adopt this charter as a common commitment to dialogue and cooperation... It is designed to promote an ecumenical culture of dialogue and cooperation at all levels of church life, and to provide agreed criteria for this... Its authority will derive from the voluntary commitments of the European churches and ecumenical organisations."

The language is neither dogmatic nor purely legalistic. But the seriousness of the document is completely clear. For someone who does not have the right spirit and readiness for dialogue, there is no language or formulation which would be more helpful. We know very well, and the drafting committee often discussed it, that the German word "Verpflichtung" (commitment) and

"Wir verpflichten uns" (We commit ourselves) might be variously translated, in the various European languages, by concepts which do not always mean exactly that: some might be stronger and some less strong. Nevertheless, the intention of the document must be understood!

Part I of the document, too, manifests clearly the undaunted determination to bring about visible unity. "We believe in 'one holy catholic and apostolic church'", we confess together in the words of the one ecumenical confession of faith, from the Second Ecumenical Council, held in Constantinople in 381. Here too the intention is clear. In this confession of faith we have a common foundation; it is, still today, the text that binds us together in mutual obligation. It is the "definition" of the church which we all recognise, "one, holy, catholic and apostolic", properly understood and properly interpreted. The word "catholic" is not the later, confessional concept, which excludes, but rather the concept from the early church which is common to all of us, which is all-embracing, which expresses the qualitative depth and the quantitative breadth, in time and space, of the mysterium ecclesiae. This can serve to clear away and overcome both the fears among the Protestant confessions of being "taken over" by the Roman Catholic Church, and the confessional exaggerations on the Catholic side, inferring that "catholic" might mean just their actual church. Here we have a lot of work to do in convincing the one side and the other, because both carry the burden and the hardening they have endured from this concept and will be difficult, psychologically in any case, to persuade.

"Called together to unity in faith". In this first chapter we read: "With the Gospel of Jesus Christ, according to the witness of Holy Scripture and as expressed in the ecumenical Nicene-Constantinopolitan Creed of 381, we believe in the Triune God: the Father, Son and Holy Spirit. Because we here confess 'one, holy, catholic and apostolic church' our paramount ecumenical task is to show forth this unity, which is always a gift of God.

"Fundamental differences in faith are still barriers to visible unity. There are different views of the church and its oneness, of the sacraments and ministries. We must not be satisfied with this situation. Jesus Christ revealed to us on the cross his love and the mystery of reconciliation; as his followers, we intend to do our utmost to overcome the problems and obstacles that still divide the churches."

This is indeed the heart of this manifestation of undaunted determination to do everything possible to overcome the ecumenical problems which we have. And the Charta Oecumenica states the problem very honestly and openly: "There are different views of the church and its oneness." This brief sentence merely indicates the various problems, for the purpose was not to deal with ecclesiological difficulties here. The ecclesiological issue must be treated more intensively by the churches together. The document emphasises that "We must not be satisfied with this situation." This sentence indicates the perception that there are indeed problems, but manifests the firm determination to keep working on them. On the Catholic side there was formerly complete clarity. Its firm and unshakeable ecclesiological self-understanding did not even allow it to consider membership in the World Council of Churches. The ecclesiological issue, as it is now also being approached by the WCC Faith and Order Commission, together with the CEC Commission "Churches in Dialogue", must be thoroughly investigated. If not, we will mean different things by the same concept and thus be talking past one another.

This issue is strongly connected with the next: what is the unity which we want? There are various views and concepts and models[1]. Here I would like to make some brief comments from an Orthodox viewpoint.

In the Orthodox view, the unity of the church is never seen as fixed uniformity, and we have never demanded such a unity. For the Orthodox Church, a koinonia ton ekklesion, a fellowship of sister churches is the goal, in an abundant plurality of forms, which does not detract from unity, but rather enriches the fellowship.

But there is one question which must be asked: Where do the boundaries lie between the necessary unity of the faith and the meaningful, legitimate and necessary diversity of the church?[2] This question is certainly not easy to answer, and this is not the place to do it. But one thing can be said with certainty: it would be ill-considered, and would not help us in gaining clarity, if we allowed everything, that is, every interpretation and conception

---

[1] Most recently: Kirchengemeinschaft nach evangelischem Verständnis. Ein Votum zum geordneten Miteinander bekenntnisverschiedener Kirchen (A Protestant Understanding of Fellowship Among Churches; a vote for well-ordered relations among churches of different confessions). By the Council of the Evangelical Church in Germany (EKD), Herrenhäuser Straße 12, 30419 Hannover, Germany (EKD Texte 69), Hannover 2001.

[2] Cf.: G. Larentzakis, "Vielfalt in der Einheit aus der Sicht der Orthodoxen Kirche (Diversity in Unity from the Viewpoint of the Orthodox Church). Versuch einer Selbstdarstellung", in: Ökumenisches Forum 8(1985)65ff. See also G. Larentzakis, *Die Orthodoxe Kirche. Ihr Leben und ihr Glaube* (*The Orthodox Church: Its Life and its Faith*), Styria Verlag, Graz Wien Köln 2001.

someone might think of as the content of the Good News of Jesus Christ, to stand as meaningful and legitimate diversity. Even if such an attitude could be imagined under the cloak of tolerance or of peace, or even of making church unity practicable, it could not be accepted, because diversity does not in itself guarantee that the content is always identifiable as the Christian Gospel, that it always offers direction and guidance for the life and the salvation of humankind. Here, Gregory of Nazianzus is surely right in saying, "For us, peace does not have a higher standing than the Word of Truth; we will not make a concession merely in order to be known as tolerant."[3] And Protestant theologian Adolf-Martin Ritter says: "These maxims should become rules for all those to whom pastoral care and the administration of the precious Word of God is entrusted!"[4]

Unity in plurality or diversity is nothing new, from the Orthodox viewpoint. The church has existed legitimately and meaningfully in this way since early in its first millennium - in diversity amongst local churches and diversity in the autonomous administration of the regional churches, as affirmed by the ecumenical councils in which all churches took part; hence the later eastern and western patriarchates. There has been diversity, too, in the many liturgies and liturgical orders: the richness of forms for celebrating the Holy Eucharist, the liturgies of Alexandria, of Antioch, and of St. James, St. Basil and St. John Chrysostom in the East, and in the West the Roman, Gallic, Mozarabic and African liturgies, and so forth. But all those who practised these believed that they were only doing what Jesus expressed as a final wish: "Do this in remembrance of me," and "This is my body," "This is my blood." That means that the essence of each form belonged to the indispensable faith which we share. In theological debate also, and in ways of depicting the Christian faith, there has from the beginning been a rich diversity of concepts and forms of expression, for the important thing was not the concepts but the saving content of the faith. On this the great fathers of the church agreed: Athanasius, Basil, Gregory of Nazianzus, and others. This is the view and the firm conviction of the Orthodox Church to this day. And in this we also see an important task for us: we must find one another again in the essential content of our faith, our Christian faith, in what it means to be a Christian as such.

We must therefore fulfil the commitment in the Charta Oecumenica which says: "We commit ourselves...in the power of the Holy Spirit, to

---

[3] Gregory of Nazianzus, *Farewell Address*, 42, PG 36, 473A.
[4] A.-M. Ritter, *Das Konzil von Konstantinopel und sein Symbol (The Council of Constantinople and Its Creed)*. Göttingen 1965, p. 266.

work towards the visible unity of the Church of Jesus Christ in the one faith, expressed in the mutual recognition of baptism and in eucharistic fellowship, as well as in common witness and service."(1) We also commit ourselves, in the spirit of the Charta Oecumenica, to pursue our dialogue conscientiously and intensively (6), for "in order to deepen ecumenical fellowship, endeavours to reach a consensus in faith must be continued at all cost. Only in this way can church communion be given a theological foundation. There is no alternative to dialogue."

On the Way Towards the Visible Fellowship of the Churches in Europe

Waclaw Hryniewicz

Centuries of not living in communion have strongly marked our confessional identity. We are still victims of historical conflicts, denominationalism and other forms of ecclesiastical competition. To remember who we are is not enough. One has to ask above all: "Whose are we?" We all belong to Christ. Ecumenism educates us to discover an open, fuller and wiser identity. "We belong together in Christ", says the Charta Oecumenica, echoing the words of the Apostle: "alive or dead we belong to the Lord" (Rm 14:8). This statement is indeed "of fundamental significance in the face of our differing theological and ethical positions". It helps us to see "our diversity as a gift which enriches us".

The difficult ecumenical process of reconciliation cannot be accomplished without an ethos of compassion. We are too severe in our judgements. We think too readily of differences in our understanding of the one faith. We forget too easily that "there exists an order or hierarchy of truths" (Decree on Ecumenism, 11). Out of our controversies and disputes we have built institutionalized divisions and have acquiesced to those divisions. The Charta Oecumenica indicates the most difficult task facing Christians, which is to convert the Churches to one another in mutual understanding and trust, in compassion and forgiveness. An ecumenism of the mind is not enough. We need also an ecumenism of the heart, a truly learning and therapeutic process. It requires, as the Second Vatican Council says in its Decree on Ecumenism (art. 8), a "change of heart", conversio cordis. The Charta also stresses the role of "the renewal of our hearts and the willingness to repent and change our ways".

The divine gift of unity is stronger than our divisions

We confess the one Church of God - the Church of Christ and of the Holy Spirit. "For by one Spirit we are all baptized into one body" (1 Co 12:13). The unity with which God endowed his Church is a reality rooted in the mystery of the divine life itself. Divisions in the church do not reach its mysterious depths. The divided Church remains the one Church of the risen Lord in the history of humanity. Divisions affect its visible historical reality so that communion cannot find its perceptible expression. They obscure and distort the visible image of the one Church, but the deepest nature of God's gift remains untouched. Human sins are not able to destroy the reality which comes from God himself and which he sustains.

That is why the innermost roots of the unity of the Church have never been damaged. This truly divine core remains a bright reality even amidst an imperfect communion of the Churches. Christ's promise that the Church cannot be destroyed (cf. Mt 16:18; 28,20) is the source of hope that no division will ever manage to destroy its essential unity. It is at the same time a continuous call to reconciliation and mutual recognition. All the commitments of the Charta Oecumenica encourage concrete steps in this direction. They urge Christians "to acknowledge the spiritual riches of the different Christian traditions, to learn from one another and so to receive these gifts", "to deepen the spiritual fellowship among the churches".

As God's gift, the unity of the Church is stronger than any division caused by human decisions. Ecumenical efforts consist first in rediscovering in divided Christianity the essential unity that already exists, given once and for all by God, and, second, in making that unity visible through the restoration of full Eucharistic communion. All the essential notes of the Church ("one, holy, catholic and apostolic") constitute a historical task to be constantly accomplished. As weak and sinful human beings we fail in relation to each one of them: to its unity, holiness, catholicity and apostolicity, thus diminishing the credibility of the Church in the world.

One can hear quite often nowadays a sad observation: "The world is changing - enmity and hatred remain". When the Churches contribute to enlarging the degree of hostility among people it is indeed a negation of their credibility and mission. The Good News of God's love for all as proclaimed by Jesus is turned thus into disrepute. It was Jesus Christ who "in his own person killed the hostility" (Eph 2:16). A competitive kind of evangelization, which has no real concern for reconciliation between Christians is simply dishonest and false. A true evangelization brings peace, gives courage and hope in the human quest for meaning. We are not allowed to export our divisions and rivalries with our proclamation of the Gospel.

To overcome division in oneself

Ecumenism is a sort of beneficial education for all of us. It aims at educating believers in such a way that there are more and more Christians inwardly free from the chains of division and separation. Fortunately, there are Christians who live and act according to the inner law of grace and freedom, in a truly Christian way. One can only rejoice that this is so. It is indeed a victory of the spirit of Christ's Beatitudes over the spirit of a narrow and unfeeling denominationalism, which so often hurts people. Ecumenism teaches how to overcome the state of split and schism in oneself above all. I believe that such a desire for reconciliation and unity can exist, inwardly delivering those who have this longing for unity from the state of separation.

Early Christianity knew the so-called "baptism of desire". The belief in its existence originated in a very difficult period of history when sometimes baptism of water was physically impossible. The death that martyrs suffered for Christ was considered to be a "baptism of blood". Others who could not receive baptism "through water and the Spirit" (Jn 3:5) but longed for it were believed by Christians to have received baptism by their desire.

This concept may offer a certain ecumenical analogy. The strong wish for unity can be fulfilled in a situation in which, though sharing the basic truths of the Christian faith, the Churches are not yet able and ready to overcome division and acknowledge themselves mutually as Churches. I believe this desire for unity is a kind of inner personal anticipation of a reconciled diversity. It achieves in the heart of a Christian something that our Churches, for various reasons, are not yet able to achieve. He or she becomes then a human being inwardly free from impoverishing division and separation. Remaining loyal to his or her Church they recover a living consciousness of belonging together in Christ and to be members of His Church. They rediscover their deep spiritual fellowship with other Christians. We still seem to be too pusillanimous and helpless in the face of divisions, and not ingenious enough. This diminishes our possibilities to proclaim the Gospel together, to move towards one another, to pray and act together, to reach a consensus in faith through patient dialogue.

We will not give up hope

We live in a difficult period of transition marked by conflicts and tensions between the Churches. Quite recently a voice was heard in my country: "Ecumenists, give up every hope", "Churches and faith will still divide us for a long time", "For the majority of us Christ is no Teacher, but only an incantation 'to ward off evil'". This situation should not become a reason for discouragement. It should rather urge us to see more clearly the acute need to overcome the feelings of mistrust, antipathy, self-sufficiency and division - first of all in oneself. Within the civil society people are able to reach agreements on a cultural, social and political level. The very process of Europe's integration encourages us to be more ingenious and creative in overcoming our divisions. Cultural polyphony often seems today to outdo religious polyphony. We can be grateful to God, however, for in this way He arouses in us a sense of urgency, or even makes us feel ashamed through the example of the civil sphere.

Ecumenically minded Christians do not and will not give up the hope to lower the ecclesiastical walls that separate us from one another. We realize how difficult this task is. Our Churches still tend to increase their doctrinal and practical claims. It is often the result of a narrow understanding of the truth, and of the lack of confidence in the guidance of the Holy Spirit. Ecumenism educates to another style of thinking, feeling and acting, as described in the Charta Oecumenica. If we do not become more humble in the face of the divine truth, which is above all Christ in person (cf. Jn 14:6), a shortsighted denominational education will further prevail over ecumenical openness and readiness to understand the others. Whoever is liberated from the chains of inner division is not a dreamer, but makes this world a bit brighter and worthier of God. Ecumenical hope, by no means naïve, allows us to live and to labour for the future of a more reconciled Christianity.

Our Common Responsibility in Europe

Reinhard Frieling

The President of the European Union (EU), Romano Prodi, speaking at a reception for church representatives, expressed appreciation for the churches' contribution to the process of European unification, and then added meaningfully, as an expectation for the future: "We need your voice, but please, not as separate voices, but as the trinity of Catholic, Orthodox and Protestant traditions!"

On the principle that "there is strength in unity", this judgment by Prodi the politician is not only understandable, but is surely also worth taking to heart by the churches. A common position taken by the churches has more weight in political councils than a whole series of church positions, since politicians don't know how to evaluate and categorise the latter properly. Certainly a common position requires the churches to reach a consensus on the content of particular issues, and that they be able to formulate this consensus together and also to represent and support it jointly vis-à-vis the political authorities. Many ecumenical studies and statements - not least of all those from the two European Ecumenical Assemblies in Basel (1989) and Graz (1997) - provide documentary evidence that there is a basic Christian consensus on most of the relevant social issues. The Charta Oecumenica itself, in its Part III (Nos. 7-12), describes some Christian principles held in common which the churches want to employ in helping to build Europe, which could in fact meet Prodi's expectations.

On the other hand is the sober realisation that the churches are only "on the way towards the visible fellowship of the churches in Europe", as the title of Part II of the Charta Oecumenica has it, and that our ability to speak with one voice has yet to be developed. The reality of parallel and sometimes competing confessional identities continually leads individual churches to go it alone. The hope for all the various Christian traditions to be melted down into an institutional unity is about as realistic as the prospect for a general renunciation of sovereignty by all the European Union member states in favour of the EU.

Certainly we must count on the existence of churches of different confessions, and with different national structures, for a long time to come. But in the Charta Oecumenica and its "Guidelines for the Growing Cooperation among the Churches in Europe" we have a hope that common ecumenical structures as well, such as councils of churches, will slowly but surely gain the confidence and the mandate of the churches to speak on their behalf, on common concerns, with one voice. If the churches take seriously the commitment in No. 4 of the Charta Oecumenica, we will come a step closer to this goal: "We commit ourselves to act together at all levels of church life wherever conditions permit and there are no reasons of faith or overriding expediency mitigating against this." With these words, the Charta Oecumenica offers some prospects for the churches to participate in building Europe.

Proclaiming the Gospel in word and deed

The Charta lifts up, as areas of joint responsibility for us, the themes of the so-called "conciliar process" for peace, justice and the integrity of the creation (Nos. 7-9), and in view of the secularisation and religious pluralism of Europe today it also contains commitments to dialogue with other religions in Europe (Nos. 10-12). This should move us to look into the question of what the specific Christian witness is which the churches want to bring to Europe in its process of unification. Do the churches have a specific Christian conception of Europe?

The Charta avoids trying to bring back old ideas of a "Christian Europe" or of the "Christian soul" of Europe. These concepts are laden with the negative experiences of history since the early Middle Ages, because they often connected the Gospel less with service to human society than with the churches' striving for hegemony in the struggle for political power. In the historical unity of empire and church, of imperium and sacerdotium, lie the intellectual and spiritual roots of imperialist thinking which, in Europe (especially in the West) and beyond - for example through the Crusades, the persecution of heretics and confessional wars, slavery, and Christianisation by force in the often unholy combination of mission and colonisation - often did not bring blessing, but rather suffering and guilt.

On the other hand, the Charta Oecumenica rightly says in No. 7: "Through the centuries Europe has developed a primarily Christian character in religious and cultural terms... We are convinced that the spiritual heritage of Christianity constitutes an empowering source of inspiration and enrichment for Europe." Before it speaks of strategic considerations for politics and for church policies, as to how the churches are to raise their voice together in the midst of the plurality of different forces in European society, the Charta Oecumenica mentions two focal issues which are central to all the rest. "The most important task of the churches in Europe is the common proclamation of the Gospel, in both word and deed, for the salvation of all." (No. 2). And secondly: "Our faith helps us to learn from the past, and to make our Christian faith and love for our neighbours a source of hope for morality and ethics, for education and culture, and for political and economic life, in Europe and throughout the world." (No. 7).

These words show our acceptance of Europe, in its plurality of world views and cultures, as the historical setting of the Christian witness. The Christian "concept of Europe" consists primarily of preserving for, or communicating to, this Europe with its people, nations, political structures and civil societies, the common values which for us Christians, in the light of the Gospel of Jesus Christ, surpass all other world views. Our powers of persuasion have only two means available: the Word, argued with faith and reason, and with no other force used, and our own exemplary lives as Christians and as churches, to communicate something of God's presence to others.

In planning for the Europe of the future, Christians pick up the positive values from our tradition, for example the development of fundamental human freedoms and rights based on our belief that all people are made in God's image; great works of art (painting, architectural monuments, literature and music); and the building of health facilities and social welfare services in the spirit of Christian love of one's neighbour. With the Charta Oecumenica, Christians and churches together will seek ways, through the civil society as well as the European political institutions, for space to be kept available for the churches, church groups and individual Christians to carry on their work in fulfilment of their responsibility towards the world, thus contributing effectively to the so-called "soul for Europe".

The Charta Oecumenica does not call for special privileges for churches, but rather encourages them to exercise their right, within democratic societies conceived on the principle of subsidiarity, to develop their proclamation of the Gospel through word and deed, freely and as far as possible through ecumenical agreement or cooperation. And it emphasises that we are ready "to be open to dialogue with all persons of good will, to pursue with them matters of common concern, and to give proof to them of our Christian faith." (No. 12)

The churches, the nations and Europe

Before beginning to speak of some actual tasks to be done in Europe today, the Charta mentions two aspects which constitute a challenge, both for the churches and for the ecumenical movement in Europe: "Europe" always means all of Europe, "from the Atlantic to the Urals, from the North Cape to the Mediterranean"; also highlighted is the churches' contribution to "reconciling peoples and cultures", which in turn leads to working for peace, justice and the integrity of creation.

It is appropriate here to recall some history, in order to get a realistic view of the possibilities for, and the limitations of, the churches' involvement in European unification.

For centuries we saw Europe not so much as one continent, but rather as divided into a Byzantine East, with the Orthodox churches, and a West under the influence of the Roman Catholic Church and the churches of the Reformation. Differing systems of philosophy and law have influenced these two cultures, as well as the churches and their theologies, and still today are seen, from time to time, partly as foreign and keeping us apart and partly as mutually enriching.

Overall, everywhere in Europe, churches have been closely connected with national cultures. The churches became "cultural factors" through their influence, for example, on "Catholic Poland", "Orthodox Russia" or "Lutheran Scandinavia". Even the widespread secularisation and disappearance of the church's effect on public life in most European countries has not removed these cultural influences. At the same time the churches became themselves "products of culture", since for example French Catholicism, Greek Orthodoxy and German Protestantism are today each still characterised by a certain mentality and spirituality.

Both these challenging aspects of the churches' calling have led the churches in recent decades to new reflections on the relations among homeland, nation, people, state and church. The Charta Oecumenica picks up on the conclusions from these studies in two commitments: "to resist any attempt to misuse religion and the church for ethnic or nationalist purposes" (No. 7) and "to counteract any form of nationalism which leads to the oppression of other peoples and national minorities", as well as "to work for...the non-violent resolution of conflicts" (No. 8). This may at first glance appear to be something we can take for granted, but the recent conflicts in the Balkans and Northern Ireland show that these problems are still current ones, and that the churches still have an important task of reconciliation before them. Now and then ethnic conflicts become laden with religious ideas that go beyond those of the official churches. The churches must not consider themselves powerless and resign themselves to this, but rather must bear witness together that Christians and the churches have committed their loyalty to Christ, and that all other ethnic and cultural loyalties are secondary for them.

In this spirit the churches, like no other organisations in Europe, have not only the job but also the opportunity of effectively reconciling peoples and cultures, for example through networks of encounters and partnerships, through international cooperation in social service, through "round table conversations" and conflict resolution commissions, through joint studies such as the "healing of memories". It is to be hoped that the general suggestions and commitments of the Charta Oecumenica will take concrete forms in the individual churches and countries and result in joint ecumenical actions. The experience should be made use of, that Europe does not begin outside one's own country, but can be encountered in the form of numerous foreigners and foreign churches in one's immediate neighbourhood.

Working for justice in Europe

The churches are not in a position to propose concrete strategies and concepts for the economy and politics. But it is part of the church's message to tell the politicians and entrepreneurs in no uncertain terms that a Common Market which is ruled only by so-called laissez-faire capitalism has to be corrected, because in the long run it accepts mass poverty in human society. If the entrepreneurs have only the profits of their own companies in view, with no consideration for social and ecological consequences or for fatal repercussions in other countries, Christians must demand laws in Europe which prevent this. If politicians think only of the well-being of their own nation and do not understand their political responsibility in the context of so-called "world politics", Christians must vote these politicians out of office. A European Union which is widening its internal market by bringing other European states into membership must have as its goal a social welfare market economy and not just a free market, and must share in responsibility for seeing that Europe does not develop into "an integrated West and a disintegrated East". Christians and churches must also "heighten Europe's sense of responsibility for the whole of humanity, particularly for the poor all over the world". (Charta Oecumenica, No. 7)

A further eminently important task for the churches' common witness is described in the Charta Oecumenica, No. 9, "Safeguarding the creation". In ecology and bioethics, Europe does not stand alone before the great challenge of developing "criteria for distinguishing between what human beings are scientifically and technologically capable of doing and what, ethically speaking, they should not do". Our responsibility before God calls for a common witness of the churches to the unique worth of every human being as God's creature, and the same goes for the commitment in the Charta Oecumenica to concern ourselves about "sustainable living conditions for the whole of creation".

Despite all these tasks listed in the Charta Oecumenica, the churches are not making some sort of triumphalist claim to intellectual leadership in Europe. The Charta is not an ecumenical "law book" with imperatives to oppress churches and Christians and make excessive demands on them. The form of self-commitment of a "charta" breathes, instead, the spirit of freedom, rooted in faith in the Triune God and proving itself in responsibility towards the world as obedience to faith. In view of the reality of a large number of independent churches, and a plurality of theologies and socio-ethical frameworks in the churches, the Charta Oecumenica with its common expressions is a hugely encouraging document. It is the first text in a thousand years to belong to all the churches of Europe.

So, with this ecumenical Basic Text, the question with which we began must be asked anew: how the churches can take the common concerns to which they bear witness and together bring them to acceptance in the society and the political institutions.

With one voice?

There is no doubt that it is important for each individual Christian to be inspired by the self-commitment of the churches to make his or her contribution to shaping the society. It is also important for the ecumenical movement to grow up from the "grass roots", and that the working of the Charta Oecumenica be decided essentially by its acceptance and implementation in the churches and communities of the various countries and regions. Equally important is the issue of ecumenical structures - what common instruments the churches have to permit them to speak with one voice and to act together in Europe.

This question can be answered only by a differentiated answer. It involves, on the one hand, an issue which has not yet been solved, theologically and ecclesiologically, within the ecumenical community, that of church order and the authority of church offices. Thus neither the Conference of European Churches (CEC) nor the Council of European Bishops' Conferences (CCEE) is doctrinally or legally empowered to speak with binding authority on behalf of the churches. On the other hand, the Charta Oecumenica with its guidelines illustrates that much more cooperation among the churches in Europe is possible than has yet been realised.

At present, CEC and CCEE are surely the best instruments through which to carry this out. Nevertheless, both suffer from the lack of inclination on the part of doctrinal authorities within the churches to give these organisations a clear mandate to act on their behalf, at least with regard to all the challenges in Europe which do not require a "doctrinal authority". One reason for this reticence is that most European churches are either large majority churches or small minority churches, which are only slowly beginning to build up ecumenical relations and structures within their own countries. The ecumenical community among the ecumenical individuals from these churches is making progress, but within the churches overall ecumenical responsibility within and for Europe is not a high priority. In addition there is a certain imbalance between East and West, since the churches in the EU states are confronted, by the political weight of the EU, with particular issues which are not present in the same way to the other churches and countries.

For over forty years CEC has played an outstanding role as a bridge between East and West and between Orthodoxy and Protestantism. Realistically, however, most of the CEC member churches, certainly for their own good reasons, fulfil their responsibilities towards Europe independently and speak with their own voices, and only turn to CEC if it can be of service in helping them fulfil their own responsibilities.

The Roman Catholic Church maintains church-state relations under international law, since the Vatican as a sovereign state concludes agreements on behalf of the Catholic dioceses within a state, maintains nunciatures (embassies) and is also represented by a nuncio to the EU. CCEE, however, has authority only for the concerns of pastoral ministry - which certainly covers ecumenical cooperation in Europe. However, CCEE is reluctant to allow its own clear stance, already fully developed in the context of the world-wide Roman Catholic Church, to be relativised by too much ecumenical closeness to other churches and to CEC, when these churches and their ecumenical bodies are still struggling towards a common position.

The Charta Oecumenica (No. 4) mentions the need "to strengthen cooperation between the Conference of European Churches and the Council of European Bishops' Conferences and to hold further European Ecumenical Assemblies". These are important first steps in avoiding competition and duplication of efforts, and through growing trust also in reaching the point of discussing plans and taking action together. But the vision of a European ecumenical council of all Christian churches, with a binding mandate to speak on behalf of all Christians and churches, will remain a dream for a long time to come.

III. THE CHARTA OECUMENICA - AN ECUMENICAL AGENDA FOR CHURCHES IN EUROPE

Testimonies and Experiences from the Life of the Charta Oecumenica[1]

Sarah Numico

On 22 April 2001, when we concluded the European Ecumenical Encounter in Strasbourg, entitled "I am with you always...", with the signing of the Charta Oecumenica and the sending out of the 200 delegates carrying it, a chain of prayer was already linking together the myriad cities of Europe. A month earlier, letters had gone out to all the churches, Bishops' Conferences, religious communities and movements throughout Europe from the CCEE and CEC secretariats, inviting them to pray for the European Ecumenical Encounter and for reconciliation among Christians. It was suggested that they do this during liturgies and worship celebrations in their local communities on Saturday 21 and Sunday 22 April, and the following prayer was proposed for everyone in common:

O God, King of the ages, and Creator of all creatures,
receive our prayer we offer as Christians and churches throughout Europe,
send down the gifts of Your Holy Spirit upon us,
and sanctify us through the grace of Your Son, our risen Lord Jesus Christ
who promises us, "Lo, I am with you always."
Forgive us our divisions and let us not become accustomed
to those things that divide us,
and bring us together in Your holy, catholic and apostolic
church.
By Your power, O Lord, gather us all under the authority of Your Son,
that we may praise Your Holy name and bring the good news of Your
kingdom

---

[1] This article presents some testimonies and experiences which we in CCEE have witnessed. We are aware that a great many other things are going on in Europe. But it is not yet time to add them up or to risk making syntheses; the Charta is still too recent.

to all people.
Help us, God, to build together peace and reconciliation
among all nations of our continent,
and to preserve Your creation for our children's children,
that the purpose of Your loving-kindness may be fulfilled
and that the world may know You, the one true God,
and Him whom You have sent, even Jesus Christ.
Amen

Often, in the course of the months since the signing, we in the CCEE secretariat have been saying that the "secret of the success" of the Charta Oecumenica is deeply rooted in this act of faith in God which the Charta process represents, this amazing treaty on the ecumenical journey of the churches in Europe.

"Thank you for sending us the Romanian translation of the Charta Oecumenica. We are sending it immediately to the members of the Romanian Orthodox community who are having a meeting at Nancy. I am also sending it to a small Carmelite monastery which follows the Carpathian Eastern rite," said a letter from France, 8 February 2002.

"There will be a Pax Christi team at the peace pavilion at Lourdes from May to October 2002, to welcome pilgrims and visitors. We would like to make the Charta Oecumenica available to them for information in all the languages in which it exists" (letter from France, March 2002).

"We have pleasure in sending you the translation of the Charta Oecumenica into Hungarian which has been made by a joint committee of the Hungarian Bishops' Conference and the Ecumenical Council of Churches in Hungary" (letter of 5 December 2001).

"At the Chemin Neuf (New Road) community where I am a member, every Thursday we observe a time of ecumenical prayer for Christian unity. At this time we regularly read a passage from the Charta Oecumenica and pray for the purposes it proposes. This summer at a meeting of members of the community, the Charta was introduced and distributed to everyone" (letter of 1 October 2001).

"Please send me two copies of the Charta in German, one for myself and one for a friend, for our information and for study purposes" (letter of 23 July 2001).

"The Diocesan Council of the Archdiocese of Munich and Freising is organising a meeting in Alsace in September 2001, jointly with the

Diocese of Évry-Corbeil-Essonnes in France, with which we are twinned, and we would like to devote a day to the Charta Oecumenica."

"We received the Charta Oecumenica in May, and we are very happy to see this courageous step forward. Of course the contents of the Charta still have to be put into practice. We are planning a worship celebration based on the Charta for the day of Pentecost; we have decorated a wall in our church with photographs and images based on its sub-themes; we have distributed the Charta on various occasions, and we spent a whole weekend reflecting on it with our ecumenical pastoral council" (letter of 22 June 2001).

"In the daily newspaper La Croix of 15 May, I read an article by P. Daniel Olivier affirming that the Charta Oecumenica will make progress possible towards Christian unity. The article says that the Charta is now being distributed at the local level in order to set concrete initiatives in motion. I am interested in such a course and would like to be involved in such local implementation: whom may I contact?" (letter of 15 May 2001).

This is just a small sample of the many responses which CCEE and CEC have received from the most diverse places in Europe. But what has been happening since that day, 22 April 2001, when the Charta was handed over to the 200 participants in the Encounter, so that they could be its ambassadors, witnesses and promoters?

The Charta is discussed

We have received 30 translations of the Charta - from Russian to Armenian, Esperanto and even Arabic (this last was really a surprise!). It is impossible to list the many occasions and diverse contexts and formats in which the text has been published - on Internet sites, in magazines, brochures, books, Power Point presentations... Also impossible to count are the meetings at which the Charta has been presented, or to which we have been invited. Some of these events have particularly impressed us.

Almost all the Bishops' Conferences, many councils of churches, synods, and assemblies of churches have discussed the theme of the Charta in plenary sessions (for example in Croatia, Poland, Scandinavia, Germany and Italy), and have more or less planned to take it into account in their ecumenical programmes. A "first fruit" of the Charta has been to make new encounters possible. Thus in Bosnia-Herzegovina in July 2001, the ecumenical commission of the Bishops' Conference devoted its meeting to the Charta Oecumenica and its relevance and importance for that country. The result was an invitation to the Orthodox bishops of Bosnia for a joint discussion on the text. In many faculties of theology and ecumenical institutes (Poland, Croatia, Italy, Slovakia...) the Charta Oecumenica is now the subject of ecumenical training courses, and of research and doctoral studies. Many publications also have been based on the Charta, such as the text published by the ecumenical commission of the German Bishops' Conference at Augsburg which sees it as parallel with certain statements by Catholic Church leaders on ecumenism.

The Albanian Bishops' Conference, the Albanian Orthodox Church and the Evangelical Alliance held a colloquy on the Charta Oecumenica, 28 October 2001 at the European Peace Centre in Scutari. There were about a hundred participants, people involved in the ecumenical movement including young Orthodox theological students. CCEE General Secretary Aldo Giordano was one of the speakers. On 29 October a national and a local television station jointly presented a round table discussion on the colloquy and the theme of the Charta. This meeting, we were later informed, created something of a sensation in the three churches and their relations with one another. It became possible to find more occasions for dialogue and for meetings, thus there are now exchange visits between seminarians and professors from the various faculties of theology.

Italy has been very active in promoting the Charta process. The Bishops' Conference was persistent in making its bishops and priests familiar with the Charta content, and with making it influential in the regular ministry of the local churches; study days and meetings were called for, to read and reflect on it in detail at every level and to bring it to life in ecumenical worship. Local ecumenical forums on the Charta have been organised to study possibilities for meeting and working together in such areas as the Word of God and evangelisation, common prayer, works of charity, spirituality, healing of memories and of languages. Efforts are being made to express the Charta commitments through concrete forms of inculturation and mutual service, and to give the commitments an important place in pastoral ministry with youth, in educational associations and in assemblies and communities of laypersons. A high point in the Charta process in Italy was a big national convention in early November 2001 of which the Charta was the subject, with around 300 delegates from dioceses joining in ecumenical participation. In the meantime a national Catholic, Protestant and

Orthodox commission has undertaken a joint study of the Charta, to decide on possible shared initiatives.

We receive news of such initiatives from every part of the continent. The Council President for International Relations of the Evangelical Lutheran Church of Denmark officially informed CEC, in a letter of 14 November 2001, that the Charta Oecumenica was on the agenda for discussion at meetings of the Ecumenical Council of Denmark. His church itself had then decided to pursue more detailed study of the Charta together with other churches.

When the Charta Oecumenica had been translated into Romanian, the Patriarch of the Romanian Orthodox Church sent it to all his bishops, inviting them to study it and to send him the fruits of their reflections at the Patriarchate in Bucharest. The Charta text was also published in the newsletters and magazines of the Catholic dioceses. In August 2001 there was a meeting of Romanian youth to discuss the Charta.

Countries with a longer ecumenical tradition, such as Austria, Switzerland and Germany, are also deeply involved in the process. The EKD Council, at its meeting in May 2001, described the Charta as a "helpful document for strengthening ecumenical cooperation" in Europe, and made a series of recommendations to the EKD member churches. All Protestant churches in Germany were urged to organise joint consultations with other churches before the autumn of 2002, to discuss how the statements and commitments in the Charta Oecumenica can be put into practice.

Armenia, a country on the frontier of Europe, announced that the Supreme Spiritual Council of the Armenian Apostolic Church had named a commission to study the Charta Oecumenica and ways it can be applied. A Round Table meeting of Armenian churches was convened in November 2002, the first national ecumenical colloquy for Armenian youth. This meeting was a "historic" occasion for the churches and religious communities of Armenia. For me personally as well, this trip and this encounter on the frontier of Europe was a particularly rich moment. The debate on the Charta Oecumenica began rather timidly during the first days of the colloquy, but by the end many of the young people were asking for the text in Armenian, so that they could discuss it in future and thus participate in the course being taken today by European Christians.

Even though all the churches in Europe have, in general, welcomed this initiative and the process, some understandable and legitimate objections, of different kinds, have been expressed with regard to certain parts of the text. These extend from terms like "common prayer" or "catholicity" to what some consider to be an excessive way of "bowing down" to the European Union in the third section of the Charta.. These objections witness once again to the complexity of the ecumenical journey and the need for more kindness in trying to understand the needs and sensibilities of others.

Beyond the borders of Europe

The Week of Prayer for Christian Unity 2002, "In you is the source of life", helped to make the Charta known throughout the world, as well as bringing about a new high point of prayer and reflection on the process. The Pontifical Council for Promoting Christian Unity and the World Council of Churches had in fact asked CCEE and CEC to prepare the proposed texts for worship, which were then distributed world-wide. The text focussed particularly on Europe and on the Charta Oecumenica.

The Council of the Lutheran World Federation (LWF), at its meeting in June 2001, decided to send the Charta Oecumenica to all its member churches world-wide. In his letter accompanying this mailing, in September 2001, LWF General Secretary Ishmael Noko observed that the Charta "was found to be a valuable contribution to ecumenical reflection generally at the present stages of the ecumenical movement. It is not a program of activity but guidelines for behaviour: How do we live in an ecumenical spirit open to one another?" The LWF General Secretary closed his letter with the hope that the churches to which he was writing would study the Charta.

CCEE has sent the Charta to the Assemblies of Bishops' Conferences in other continents: the CELAM in Latin America, SECAM in Africa and FABC in Asia. From the Far East, from Hong Kong, we subsequently received this letter: "Thank you for sending me a copy of the Charta; with your permission, I would like to publish it in the FABC newsletter, so that all the bishops in Asia can read it and use it" (letter of 17 May 2002).

The Charta is officially welcomed

Since the Charta does not have any legal or dogmatic authority, but is commended to the churches and communities for their self-commitment, churches in some countries or regions of Europe have decided to express their joining in the spirit and the process of the Charta by officially signing the text.

Thus in the Netherlands, as part of the annual meeting of the Council of Churches in the Netherlands on 18 January 2002, 15 churches signed the Charta Oecumenica. On 17-18 January, before the ceremony, there was an encounter between young people and older leaders of the member churches, on the model of the one that took place in Strasbourg.

A message from Georgia was received on 28 March 2002, which said: "I am happy to let you know that the Charta Oecumenica was officially presented to some non-governmental organisations and to the press (which was well represented) on 14 February at Tbilisi. The presentation was made by representatives of the Armenian Apostolic Church and of the Catholic, Lutheran and Baptist churches, who signed the document as a sign of their common commitment, in the hope that this document's fragile force will bring forth fruits of visible communion in our country too."

The four presidents of Churches Together in England and Wales, along with the Archbishop of Canterbury, the Archbishop of Westminster (Roman Catholic), the Moderator of the Free Church Federal Council and a representative of the Council of African and Afro-Caribbean Churches each signed, on 2 June 2002, a personal covenant to pursue dialogue and ecumenical cooperation. The text of this covenant was composed on the basis of Part I of the Charta.

The churches of Hungary met on 1 October 2002 for an official celebration which included the signing of the Charta. And, just as this is being written, we have heard that the German churches are planning for a similar event to take place during the first Ecumenical Kirchentag, which will be held in Berlin, 28 May - 1 June 2003.

The Charta is beginning to be experienced

The Charta Oecumenica is considered by some to have become more widely known, distributed and discussed than any other ecumenical text. As a cardinal of the Catholic Church said, its importance is that it exists at all! It is becoming a common reference point for Christians in Europe, especially its Part III, "Our Common Responsibility in Europe". But it is not enough to discuss the text, to know what it says or to study all its theological and ecumenical implications. The churches are feeling an urgent need to take concrete actions based on the Charta, in accordance with its refrain, "We commit ourselves...". The Presidents' statement at the conclusion of the Charta says: "As Presidents of the Conference of European Churches and the Council of European Bishops' Conferences, we commend this Charta Oecumenica as a Basic Text to all the churches and Bishops' Conferences in Europe, to be adopted and adapted in each of their local contexts." And indeed we are now seeing the birth of the first consultations and experiments growing out of the Charta. This is perhaps the most difficult and delicate phase of the process.

In Croatia, following an official and festive presentation of the Charta organised by an ecumenical committee, attempts are being made to launch various projects such as publishing an ecumenical journal, regular ecumenical meetings to define joint projects, promoting interconfessional work at the local level, sharing in ecumenical worship celebrations.

In Finland, the Ecumenical Council has had the Charta translated and entrusted it to its three Commissions on Faith and Order, Unity, and Mission and Evangelisation, which have decided to organise a seminar open to the general public on the question "To what are we ready to commit ourselves?" This seminar is being held just as this is being written, and is to suggest some concrete courses of action.

In France, the Council of Churches (CECEF) has published a little folder entitled "We commit ourselves with the European Charta Oecumenica" which lists the commitments made in the Charta, proposes some opportunities through which to intensify the sharing of prayer, witness and action (such as the Year of the Bible 2003, or the centenary of the laws separating church and state, or the issue of immigration) and also proposes to make more use of some "common" instruments such as the Ecumenical Translation of the Bible (TOB), an ecumenical hymnal in French (Ensemble, a Bayard-Reveil joint publication 2002), ecumenical journals, and the joint social and inter-church services... In the same spirit, a diocese in the north of France has started a study course on re-reading history ecumenically, including visits to places recalling significant events and traumas in French history.

In Germany, the ACK has also prepared an attractive brochure for study of the Charta. This "user's guide", which comes with a presentation CD, contains basic information on the origin of the text, commentaries and suggestions on its 12 points, Bible meditations and proposals for prayers and worship services, ideas and recommendations for concrete projects and initiatives at diocesan or regional and local level, and lists tools and books on ecumenical topics.

The Apulia region in Italy began the Charta process with a large-scale ecumenical colloquy in October 2001. This meeting gave rise to the idea of using the Charta as a new stimulus to ecumenical dialogue in a region which is already very active at this level. During the Week of Prayer for Christian Unity 2002, several thousand copies of the Charta were distributed. And it was signed, by nuns at their regional assembly, by youth during an evening of prayer, singing and meditation, and by local church leaders in the serene and beautiful cathedral in Bari, filled with a congregation of "ordinary" people. The churches felt that ecumenism should enter into the everyday life of the churches. An ad hoc commission has now been set up to keep track of the process of reception of the Charta throughout the region.

Several months after the signing of the Charta at Strasbourg, a diocesan meeting of Catholic youth belonging to various movements, associations and organs was held in Milan. The purpose was to decide on concrete actions which young people could undertake with reference to the Charta. With characteristic rapidity, the youth came up with a series of practical ideas for the city: making the Bible school more ecumenical, creating chances to share personal testimonies of faith, setting up an ecumenical youth centre, planning shared celebrations and prayer services. This meeting, indeed, gave birth to the initiative which was realised in early October 2002 in Milan: a Creation Day celebration organised by young people from different churches.

If the theme of preserving the creation has been taken up and inspired joint ecumenical action in many countries, another theme in the Charta has also inspired Christians in Europe: that of the encounter and dialogue with Islam, since the tragic events of 11 September 2001. The Charta text on this theme (§ 11, Cultivating relations with Islam) is considered to be realistic and prudent, yet open and stimulating. In Italy, for example, inspired by the Charta Oecumenica, an initiative has been taken to set up a "day of dialogue with Islam", on the model of the already existing "day of Jewish-Christian dialogue".

CCEE and CEC

When we sent out the envelopes containing the first draft of the Charta to the churches and Bishops' Conferences in July 1999, none of us could have imagined that it would arouse so many meetings, debates and exchanges. This process, promoted and supported by CCEE and CEC, has given rise to its own dynamics, far beyond anything our secretariats could supervise or coordinate. The Charta Oecumenica is like a child, mysterious as it is familiar, overflowing with vitality and capabilities. Having seen it into the world, the CEC and CCEE secretariats are trying now to accompany its growth through letters to churches and Bishops' Conferences, and by participating in local meetings and supporting initiatives.

In the ninth month of the Charta, the meeting of the Joint Committee - the group with ultimate responsibility for the Charta - was an important moment. It was held in the ecumenical village of Ottmaring, 24-27 January 2002. The minutes of the meeting said that "the Charta Oecumenica is useful for confronting a series of problems which in fact exist, and it is useful in every nation for developing a growing awareness of responsibility for the whole of Europe and for ecumenism as a whole; in various countries the Charta was received 'ecumenically' and looked at by councils of churches; the part of the Charta dedicated to Islam has become particularly relevant; for Orthodox Churches in general the process is longer, but this depends more on the situation rather than any unwillingness; in some countries forums or working parties are being set up for the realisation of various points of the Charta."

On this occasion, the Joint Committee was invited to Augsburg by the civic and religious leaders of the city, including a reception in the famous Golden Hall of Augsburg City Hall. Coming into this hall, we recalled the words of Mayor Menacher two years earlier, at the signing of the Lutheran-Catholic Joint Declaration on the Doctrine of Justification on 31 October 1999: "Luther said, 'I fear we will never be closer together than we were at Augsburg', referring to the Peace of Augsburg of 1555. I hope," the mayor continued, "that he was not right about that. Work has already begun on a European Charta Oecumenica." We were struck by these confident words with regard to the Charta: they seemed rather bold to us then, as we could see how fragile and uncertain the process was which was then just beginning.

At all the CEC and CCEE meetings, from assemblies and Central Committee meetings to meetings of the general secretaries of the Bishops' Conferences and various commissions on dialogue between the two organisations, the Charta continued to have an important place on the agenda. Thus the CCEE Assembly, composed of the presidents of the 34 Bishops' Conferences in Europe, has dealt with the issue of the Charta at both of its meetings held since the Charta was signed; it has always emphasised the importance of the Charta's reception in the various countries, and called upon all the Bishops' Conferences to get involved in this.

The general secretaries' meetings in June 2001 in Prague and in 2002 in Turkey have seen a wealth of sharing on the topic of the Charta Oecumenica. It seems that all the Bishops' Conferences intended to take advantage of the opportunity offered by the Charta to make real progress on the path of reconciliation among the Christians of Europe. This is very encouraging. At the meeting of presidents of Bishops' Conferences in southeast Europe, held in Slovenia in March 2002, the Charta Oecumenica was defined as a "meeting ground" which could help the process of dialogue and reconciliation in the Balkans. At the 10th Symposium of European Roman Catholic bishops in Rome, April 2002, the Charta was also presented and distributed to the participants. The idea that youth delegates could participate in the Symposium was itself a result of the Ecumenical Encounter in Strasbourg; some young people who had been in Strasbourg were present in Rome and told of their experience. In the Litterae communionis, the CCEE quarterly newsletter, there has not been one issue in the last several months which has not mentioned the Charta Oecumenica, either in the context of CCEE's activities or in the reports from countries.

For CCEE, two episodes have particularly encouraged us to move forward on the Charta Oecumenica path: in April 2002, Pope John Paul II said to the bishops and young people gathered in Rome for the symposium: "It is becoming ever clearer that reconciliation among Christians is crucial for the credibility of the proclamation of the Gospel, as well as for building Europe. In this regard, the Charta Oecumenica for Europe, signed in Strasbourg in April 2001, marks an important step in increasing collaboration among Churches and Christian communities. I pray God that people may journey in this direction with ever greater confidence and determination."

It was encouraging to have the Holy See's approval for the Charta also on another occasion, in these words: "Ecumenical and interreligious dialogue is a specific area of our own contribution to the unification of Europe. It has been inspired and stimulated by the Holy Father's trips to Sarajevo, Romania, Ukraine, Greece, Georgia and Armenia. It found a response and follow-up in the Charta Oecumenica, adopted last year in Strasbourg." (speech by Mgr. Celestino Migliore, former Under-Secretary for Inter-State Relations, at the Third International Forum of the Alcide de Gasperi Foundation, Rome, 22-23 February 2002.) The Pope himself, at his meeting with President Prodi in November 2001, had already mentioned the Charta as a contribution to the unification of Europe.

An important opportunity to evaluate the road which has been travelled was the "Consultation on Ecumenism in Europe and the Charta Oecumenica", held in Ottmaring, Germany, 7-10 September 2002. Some 50 participants from 26 countries gathered for three days to share news and experiences with the Charta Oecumenica process in Europe and its contribution to reconciliation and to European unity, and to see how to encourage those who have difficulty in taking this process into consideration. On this occasion the Charta was called "a process, a text and a dream." In their Letter from Ottmaring, the delegates wrote: "We have been greatly encouraged by so much that we have heard from across the countries of Europe, where Churches have engaged together with the Charta in deepening and maturing relationships, and we give thanks for the evident work of the Holy Spirit. But we are also aware that the work of the Holy Spirit is even present within the difficulties and challenges which we face together, and so we can be realistic about problems already encountered or foreseen."

The delegates insisted on bringing some topics in particular to the attention of their churches: "We recognise the wide agreement among churches on the importance of some key issues: especially the focus on poverty and social exclusion in Europe, the effects of migration and refugee policies, and the environment and integrity of creation, without espousing any particular political agenda. We urge the churches to use the Charta as a basis for continuing and widespread theological dialogue, especially on the nature and mission of the Church and the sacrament of the Eucharist. We ask how strong are the bonds of communion between the churches in and beyond Europe, and how should they influence our responses to the troubled regions of Europe, the Middle East and elsewhere?"

Small steps

We believe that the longest journeys and the boldest enterprises begin and grow with small steps, with small gestures taken in faith, trusting in the creative capacity of the Holy Spirit. This can be applied to the path which has been travelled by the Charta Oecumenica, to its contribution amongst all those being made in Europe today to the growth of dialogue and cooperation among the churches of our continent. If we are willing never to give up our desire and our prayer for unity, this dream will one day become reality.

The Youth Protagonists

Petra Pajdakovic

A. Personal experience

When I was asked to write about the youth perspective of the Charta, my first reaction was fear. "How will I do it?" "Will I be able to do it?" "Is my own perspective actually representative of the youth one?" (Or do young people around me, in my country and region, have a perspective about the Charta at all) - all of these were questions running through my head. Many times in life, especially when you are young, you don't really recognise the value of some things until they are over, or at least, until you have some time gap between them and the present.

I cannot say that I was an "ecumenical expert" when I participated in the European Ecumenical Encounter (I cannot say it now either, although I know a bit more) so my experience from Strasbourg can be named as "emotional" one. I went there with an open heart, bringing simplicity and a sense of communion, as the brothers of the Taizé community taught me, which had been my biggest ecumenical experience before Strasbourg. What I didn't know was that the Strasbourg meeting would change my life and turn my feet to a new path.

The whole event, held immediately after the common celebration of Easter, was a long walk to Emmaus accompanied by Christ with great inspiration from the Holy Spirit.

I come from Croatia, a traditional Catholic country with 87% of population who consider themselves to be Catholics. This means that I had not really had many opportunities to share my faith with people from other Christian denominations. I have to admit that my everyday life seemed to be completely OK like that - I didn't really feel any need to join or start some concrete steps in building communion with others. I was like a typical member of a majority who is aware that there are some minorities around, people who are different, but who doesn't really pay a lot of attention to them. In my teenage years, while I was building my relationship with God and attitudes toward society, my country passed through painful process of becoming independent, increasing aggression and the conflict of war. My generation was raised with a strong sense of belonging to the Catholic faith and national pride, and although the dialogue between politicians and church leaders always existed, no one really encouraged us to do the same. (I have to explain here that conflict in Croatia wasn't a religious one, but it was between two nations - Croatian and Serbia - who belong to the different Christian traditions - Catholic and Orthodox).

During the Encounter, I discovered for the first time a strong feeling of having the same journey as my brothers and sisters from other Christian churches, regardless of their positions or responsibilities. Although I knew a lot in theory, this was a "life practice". A "burden of the past" has become a "chance of the future". St. Paul's words came alive:

"For you are all children of God, through faith in Christ Jesus. For as many of you as were baptised into Christ have put on Christ. There is neither Jew nor Greek, there is neither slave nor free man, there is neither male nor female; for you are all one in Christ Jesus." (Galatians 3,26-28).

I was aware that the text of Charta would still have a long way to go not only to be achieved in the future, but also to match the reality (at least where I live), yet, it was a completely new sight for me. The possibility of sharing a table (during discussions or meals) with Church leaders, being able to speak and be appreciated as an equal, encouraged and given attention - for a person as young as I was, 22 at the time, this was really remarkable.

Being a youth delegate

The word "delegate" gives a strong feeling of responsibility, which can sometimes present a big burden for a young person. In Strasbourg we were 100, coming from the Atlantic coast to the Ural, from Norway to Crete, belonging to different nations and churches, trying to present them in the best way (being delegates), but also to remain curious, open-minded and unburdened (being young).

Maybe the best example of this was given by one of our friends, Vlad, from Romania who was asked to say who Jesus Christ is for him, and to

84

give something as a symbol of his faith. During this presentation, held in the Council of Europe headquarters, Vlad took out his worn-out sandals, saying that they represent all his pilgrimages, holy places he has visited, but also the journey of faith, the path which we all have to follow to enter everlasting life. No matter what nationality, language, church, race, sex, title or position, we all come to meet Christ as persons, called by our first name, and God is the one who always takes the first step. The testimony given by Cardinal Etchegaray emphasised this message which the young people wanted to underline.

The Encounter theme: "I am with you always, till the end of the days " (Matthew 28,20) was visible in every personal meeting, testimony and dialogue. It encouraged everybody to seek first what we have in common, how can we combine our differences, while searching for Christ, building community and acting together in everyday life. We felt completely equal during these days, with a common goal and looking for the common way to achieve it. There was a very nice description by Chris from Scotland: we are not - so to say - an "ecumenical soup", where all the elements and ingredients are blended together so they lose their taste and colour. On the contrary, in a salad you take lots of different tastes, colours, textures and smells and mix them together - but they remain the same - and in fact - the salad needs them to be together but not identical. So we made a map of Europe, to see what kind of "vegetables" can we find in different areas, and organised a "market place" to offer our own ingredients (ecumenical activities, initiatives, hopes and fears) for this unique "ecumenical salad". On the first night we built a house of stones which we brought from our homes, house to keep light and warm, our prayers and our hopes. Stones to make walls, walls to make a house in which we'll live together, share and feel at home.

During the workshops we discussed: mission and evangelisation; our contribution (as young Christians) in God's mission; ecumenical training and power of knowledge; interreligious dialogue in Europe as a continent of different religions; globalisation or global community (Oikoumene); integrity of creation; violence and peace; gender differences; information society and new technologies; migrations to Europe as a "promised land". There were also many other subjects, which the young people considered during the time we shared in two days of the youth preparatory meeting.

We concluded that each person should be aware that he/she is a church and so accept responsibility for that church. Prayer has to be at the core of every action and thought, and we have to be witnesses to our generation, sharing the knowledge we have, to those who are full of ignorance and prejudices. We always have to be ready to forgive and ask for forgiveness and we all need witnesses like the personal example of our teachers, priests and church leaders. Last, but not least, we always have to remain like children, nourishing simplicity of heart and welcoming everything with trust and positive thinking, enjoying meeting new people, things, ways of thinking and surrounding.

Church leaders and young people

The opening and closing sessions of the Encounter were shared by Catholic cardinal Karl Lehmann and Lutheran pastor Elfriede Dörr - this wasn't only their personal meeting and dialogue - they represented West and East, older and younger generation, male and female; joined together to implant the words of the Charta into a dialogue of life. We heard about the rule of St. Benedict who, speaking of internal matters of the monastery, says: "often the Lord reveals a better way to one of the younger members of the community".

Since this was the first meeting where young people were present in the same number as church leaders, searching for new visions in relationships between churches in Europe, both sides had big expectations. Ecumenism was here presented as an encounter, in the encounter and through the encounter. The encounter is a grace, beyond our planning - we cannot prepare it and it requires bravery to take steps towards another, asking questions, listening to answers, standing by our own attitudes with openness and respect for others.

Communication between generations makes something completely new because young people are open to the visions of future, which older people are capable of making true by sharing experience and support to the young who will continue what they started but could not finish. One problem is that the older often value only the results made by experts, taking things too seriously and looking for solutions on "high level". The young find much more value in a concrete fight and action, personal experience and, very often, a stubborn determination in the things that matter. One of the remarks by young people during the Encounter was that the older are often too "abstract", just talking how something should be done, declaring that others should do it but not doing it by themselves, and without giving an example which younger people can follow.

We felt very happy about the words we heard, and especially about the Charta, but we also kept the strong feeling that all of it first has to become alive in our hearts, that the words absolutely must become flesh. Ecumenism is not a matter of choice for the young people - ecumenical dialogue in concrete life situations is an absolute priority to the generation hoping to live its future in the united Europe.

During the Encounter we had a great opportunity of having a "walk to Emmaus" - one of the church leaders and one of the youth delegates shared a walk from the church to the university building where the common sessions were held. I shared my walk with Cardinal Roger Etchegaray and discovered the symbolism of being two disciples who were able to search, listen and discover Christ together, saying one to another: "Weren't our hearts burning within us, while he spoke to us along the way, and while he opened the Scriptures to us?" (Luke 24,32) Dialogue between generations is a necessity if we want to go further, with a fresh breeze, which comes from the Holy Spirit, and most often reveals through the youth.

Charta Oecumenica - becoming alive on a local level

It is significant that under the title "Charta Oecumenica" stands "guidelines for the growing cooperation among the Churches in Europe". The positive approach of this sentence, which assures that cooperation not only exists but shows as a growing process, presents a joy for every person who is involved in ecumenical dialogue and wants to know more precisely how to develop it in concrete ways. It is visible that the text comes as a result of many thoughts and initiatives which have already been proved in life, and a form of commitment showing the seriousness of the matters that Charta talks about.

Yet, although I like it a lot, my opinion is that it includes many things that are still "science fiction" in everyday life. The picture of Europe as written in the preamble - from the Atlantic to the Ural, from the North Cape to the Mediterranean - is still not a picture of reality we live in. If we would try to draw a "Christian map" of Europe, we would see that ecumenical cooperation and problems that Churches face, are different in every corner of Europe. Some of the points of Charta are already very well developed in the certain areas and among some churches, while others will have to work very hard to achieve them or they even won't matter so much.

During the Encounter I became aware that the situation and level of ecumenical dialogue in my region is very unique and different than in some other parts of Europe. If we all aspire to the building of common European household, our backgrounds and realities we bring to it sometimes present a big challenge to overcome. A very important thing, especially when involving young people in that process, is a good education and constant exchange of information. Every person should have a chance to receive a message in a language that he/she understands and be encouraged and supported to put it into reality.

Concretely, I can say that we have an honour to live in an area with the long and fruitful history of dialogue between not only Christians, but also with Islam. Even during the recent conflicts, interdenominational and interreligious dialogue was present not only among the church leaders, but also believers in local communities, especially in a form of prayers for peace, caritas and humanitarian aid etc.

There is also a significant growth of ecumenical initiatives among young people recently, especially cross-border ones, which connect youth from Croatia, Bosnia and Herzegovina and Serbia and Montenegro. With the situation where minorities from one country are majorities in another one, it shows that young people have much more sense for the problems of "small people" and desire to help in solving them. We still have to see what will be the contribution of the Charta in a process of healing the wounds and growing of the present cooperation. We still need time, patience, prayer and efforts. We need to make people understand that each one of them can make a difference. As I said in the beginning, I'm not sure that young people have a perspective of Charta as an existing document (maybe also because there wasn't paid very big attention to it in the media), but I'm sure that many of them say "we commit" with their lives and actions - and that's what makes Charta alive.

The Contribution of the Charta Oecumenica to European Construction

John Coughlan and Keith Jenkins

"The churches support an integration of the European continent. Without common values, unity cannot endure. We are convinced that the spiritual heritage of Christianity constitutes an empowering source of inspiration and enrichment for Europe. On the basis of our Christian faith, we work towards a humane, socially conscious Europe, in which human rights and the basic values of peace, justice, freedom, tolerance, participation and solidarity prevail. We likewise insist on the reverence for life, the value of marriage and the family, the preferential option for the poor, the readiness to forgive, and in all things compassion." (Charta Oecumenica § 7)

Many Christian churches in Europe demonstrate a long and active commitment to the process of building a united and peaceful Europe founded on a shared heritage and common values. They have contributed to the orientation of policy as well as to the details of legislation, and, whilst being critical when appropriate, they have consistently supported the ultimate objective of building a political and economic system, in the form of the European Union, with the vocation to promote the values laid out in the Charta Oecumenica - peace, justice, freedom, tolerance, participation and solidarity - not only in Europe but across the world. They also show commitment to other European structures which contribute to realising the values of the Charta Oecumenica - the Council of Europe and the Organisation for Security and Co-operation in Europe.

Unity in diversity

Ecumenism and the process of European integration have evolved in parallel over the last half-century. They share the common feature of seeking to bring people and communities together whilst respecting their diverse competences and identities. This concept of subsidiarity, which has its roots in Christian social thought, has become a guiding principle for the European integration process. "Unity in diversity", the motto chosen by Europe's young people to mark the 50th anniversary of European integration in 2000, has also been one of the guiding principles of the Ecumenical Movement.

The parallels between ecumenism and European integration are not coincidental. Each is born from a desire for reconciliation, a desire to heal the wounds of past divisions and to work together in order to be able to fulfil our shared mission and responsibilities. In the aftermath of the Second World War, the churches were at the forefront of the movement for reconciliation from which the process of European integration emerged. The churches have also been constant advocates for enlarging the space of peace and solidarity in Europe through the accession of the former communist states in Central and Eastern Europe to the European Union. Today the churches are prominent among those leading the call for the European Union to recognise its global responsibilities, to promote democracy and human rights, to alleviate poverty and suffering, and to develop a more just system of economic and political governance.

However, the wars in South Eastern Europe during the last decade of the twentieth century served as a painful reminder that religious differences can still be exploited for political and economic ends on our continent; and since the terrible events of 11 September 2001, we Christians are compelled more than ever to prove that our religious faith is a foundation for peace and not a source of conflict.

In a modern European society marked by both secularisation and diversity, the credibility of the Gospel message depends on our ability as Christians to work together peacefully. The commitment of the churches "to resist any attempt to misuse religion and the church for ethnic and nationalist purposes" (Charta Oecumenica § 7), and their request for forgiveness for past failures, are therefore signs of hope and an example for all. The churches' willingness to work together with Jews, Muslims and the faithful of other religious traditions on matters of common concern (Charta Oecumenica §§ 10, 11, 12) is also an invaluable testimony to peaceful coexistence.

Christian values

In a Europe of such diversity, no single creed or culture can predominate. However, the Charta Oecumenica defines the shared values that constitute the common ground between our churches and provide the foundation for our common contribution towards building a more peaceful, more just and more responsible Europe. In an interdependent world, Christian values such as "reconciling people and cultures" and "safeguarding Creation" (Charta Oecumenica §§ 8, 9) cannot be put into action unless churches, communities and nations work together. The commitment of the churches "to seek agreement with one another on the substance and goals of our social responsibility, and to represent in concert, as far as possible, the concerns and visions of the churches vis-à-vis the secular European institutions" (Charta Oecumenica § 7) is therefore a prerequisite for achieving a Christian vision of the future of Europe.

In so far as the European Union is concerned, this commitment is fulfilled through the daily co-operation between the Church and Society Commission of the Conference of European Churches (CSC-CEC), and the Commission of the Bishops' Conferences of the European Community (COMECE). It also involves co-operation with the numerous other representations of churches and Christian organisations that monitor and contribute to the work of the institutions of the Union.

Such co-operation has been particularly evident in relation to the Convention on the Future of Europe, a body of representatives from national parliaments and governments, the European Parliament and the European Commission, which was set up at the beginning of 2002 with the aim of defining the objectives, values and competences of the future European Union. Through joint letters, a common statement to the hearing of civil society and regular briefing sessions and papers for Christian organisations, the churches have been able to convey a coherent message to the members of the Convention.

COMECE and CSC-CEC in particular have a long-standing tradition of working together closely through the Dialogue Seminars, organised twice a year in co-operation with the European Commission on a topical issue on the agenda of the European Union. Permanent ecumenical networks also help the churches to contribute to the development of EU policy and legislation in specific areas, such as asylum and immigration policy and foreign and security policy.

Giving Europe a soul

The commitments of the Charta Oecumenica to work with a variety of communities of faith and conviction need to be put into effect. One practical example of this is in the "Soul for Europe - Ethics and Spirituality" Initiative. CEC and COMECE participate in this with European partners from other communities, including humanists. Originally conceived as a means of giving the European Commission expert advice on grant applications with a spiritual or ethical dimension, the Initiative is now a place of reflection between communities, exploring, through seminars and discussions, how they can contribute together on European integration.

The use in the early nineties of the phrase "Giving a Soul to Europe" by the then President of the European Commission, Jacques Delors, had an additional significance. Up to then, the process of European integration had the primarily economic objective of building a single market. It was then turning towards the goal of political union. Delors saw that this meant a redefinition of purpose and to that end he sought the co-operation of thinkers to define that purpose.

That redefinition of the central purpose has remained elusive. At the same time there has been a growing distance between citizens and political life. While this has been widespread, the European institutions and the European integration process have been a particular target of public criticism, cynicism and disillusion, evidenced by low participation in elections to the European Parliament, negative referenda results and the growth of Eurosceptic political parties, sometimes with xenophobic nationalist tendencies. In part this has been explained by the diplomatic rather than the democratic means by which the process of European integration has advanced, and to which the Convention on the Future of Europe is intended to respond.

European integration was intended to be a project of peace-building and reconciliation. That is the basis of Christian support for it. Nowadays, the churches recognise the need "to join forces in promoting the process of democratisation in Europe" (Charta Oecumenica § 8) and this involves promoting the reinvigoration of political life and the stimulation and promotion of the debate on what European integration means today.

The Charta Oecumenica is a European document. It focuses on European integration. It commits the churches to working together at the European level. But it also points to the existence of critical questions about the future of Europe and its people which need intense discussion throughout Europe and at every level. It is a document about the meaning of co-operation, fellowship and integration. That search for meaning requires a continuing ecumenical effort by the churches.

The Challenge of Interreligious Dialogue

Heinz Klautke and Hans Vöcking

In the section of the Charta Oecumenica on "Our Common Responsibility in Europe", the churches take a position on Islam and on encountering other religions and world views. Paragraph 11 says: "We would like to intensify encounters between Christians and Muslims and enhance Christian-Islamic dialogue at all levels. We recommend, in particular, speaking with one another about our faith in one God, and clarifying ideas on human rights."

Paragraph 12 says that Europe has changed with regard to religions; "Eastern religions and new religious communities are spreading and also attracting the interest of many Christians." The churches commit themselves "to recognise the freedom of religion and conscience of these individuals and communities and to defend their right to practise their faith or convictions, privately or publicly, in the context of rights applicable to all."

The Charta describes briefly the political, religious and social situation in today's Europe, which has become a challenge for the churches. Christians in Europe are today experiencing what is considered normal on other continents. Indeed, the religious geography of Europe has changed markedly in the last 30 or 40 years. The most visible changes were certainly caused by the 40 years of Communist rule, which promoted scientific atheism. Albania called itself "the first atheistic state" in the world. In other European countries, secularism has brought about atheism in practice, and large groups of people have distanced themselves from the religious traditions of their parents and grandparents.

The immigration of new work forces has been the main reason that some 12 million Muslims live in Western European countries. But Christians in central and eastern Europe have known the presence of Muslims since the 16th century, when they came under the rule of the Ottoman Empire. The political and economic situation in Asia has driven people from their homelands towards Europe. Today it is estimated that there are a million Buddhists in the countries of Europe. In the Russian Federation, Buddhism is legally recognised as one of the traditional religions, along with the Orthodox Church, Islam and Judaism.

Religions which were formerly at home only in Africa and Asia can now be observed and experienced in Europe. Philosophical movements such as humanism are organising themselves and demanding their rights. Thus it is logical that the official texts of the European Union speak of "churches, religious communities and philosophical movements". In European cities today, besides churches, mosques and Buddhist and Hindu temples can also be found. In countries which include religious instruction in the official programmes of public schools, instruction in Islam and in humanism as well as Christianity is given. In many countries the calendar now includes the feast days of the world religions. At parliamentary hearings on ethical and political problems, representatives not only of the churches but also of other religions or philosophical movements are invited and listened to.

Since the terror attacks of 11 September 2001 in New York and Washington, interreligious dialogue has become a central issue for world politics and of interest to a wide audience. Politicians and the media have rediscovered religions as a topic in politics and the society. The absolute necessity of interreligious and intercultural dialogue is invoked, and is considered indispensable for preserving world peace. What is being demanded by so many is, however, already a reality, for the churches in Europe have been active in interreligious dialogue for decades. There are also political and institutional initiatives towards interreligious dialogue; however, these make only limited use of the experience of the churches and religious communities. Thus it would make sense in future for international organisations and politicians to discuss this issue with the churches (and the other religions). They could share their experiences with dialogue and raise the consciousness of leaders and church members with regard to interreligious and intercultural dialogue.

A distinction needs to be made between interreligious and intercultural dialogue. Religion and culture influence one another, but do not necessarily coincide and may not even overlap. Even so, in political debates the two are often confused, in a way that may conceal a rhetorical strategy. This may be the case when politicians who want to preserve their own neutrality with regard to world views nevertheless seek cooperation with religious communities. They think that this conceptual change will protect them against religious prejudice. Having recourse to intercultural dialogue then becomes a way of retreating into a legitimate grey area. Attention must be paid to the subtle distinction between interreligious and intercultural dialogue when sounding out the possibilities for, and limits of, interreligious dialogue, and finding an appropriate setting for the topics to be discussed. This is especially true when politicians are to be included in an interreligious dialogue.

Interreligious dialogue is a shifting concept. It would be clearer if distinctions were made between levels of dialogue, the content of dialogue, the methods to be used, and the groups to be involved. With regard to levels, interreligious dialogue can be conducted world-wide, Europe-wide, within a nation or region, or strictly at the local level. As to the content of dialogue, clear distinctions must be made between interreligious conversations about theological positions such as ideas of God, understandings of the scriptures, revelation, ethics, and those about legal and political problems; the latter include specific issues such as religious instruction, or world problems which concern everyone, such as peace, globalisation, bioethics and preservation of the creation. Thus interreligious dialogue can be conducted along philosophical or problem-solving lines; both are necessary. There are also various methods of interreligious dialogue. It can be done as a sharing of experience among adherents of different religions, or by developing a common position on ethical questions. The highest form of interreligious dialogue is certainly that of spiritual or devotional encounter among individual believers and communities, which is practised, for example, by women and men in dialogue among monastic communities.

Attention must also be given to the setting for interreligious dialogue. A bi-lateral conversation between representatives of two religious communities has its own dynamic which is different from that of a conversation among several religious communities. It is also different from inter-confessional dialogue, as found within the Christian ecumenical family and the new intra-Islamic dialogue which has been set in motion since 11 September 2001. In the end, what is decisive for interreligious dialogue is the groups which are conducting it. It will be different, depending whether these are religious dignitaries, scholars, politicians and adherents of the different faiths, young people, women or men, because these groups are working on different areas of concern and with different goals. It also makes a difference whether people are participating who are influenced only culturally by religion, but are otherwise secular-oriented.

How then should interreligious dialogue be organised, such as the Charta Oecumenica aims to promote and intensify, on theological and socio-political issues in Europe? There is a great diversity of activities being carried out by churches and political institutions in Europe towards dialogue among religions. An example is the meeting of religious dignitaries which was organised by the Ecumenical Patriarch, Bartholomaios I, in cooperation with EU Commission President Prodi, 19-20 December 2001 in Brussels. Some 80 Jewish, Islamic and Christian representatives participated. The final declaration, "God's Peace in the World", pointed out the constructive role which religion can play in the dialogue among cultures. The participants repudiated violence in the name of religion and declared their support for interreligious and intercultural initiatives.

An example of a political effort towards interreligious dialogue is the Barcelona Conference of 1995, organised by the European Union together with the Mediterranean countries of North Africa and the Near East, for their foreign ministers, with the aim of building a particular partnership. In their closing resolution the ministers declared that interreligious and intercultural dialogue was essential to dialogue among Mediterranean peoples. There had already been preparation for this resolution at the interreligious Conference of Toledo in 1995, held jointly by the EU Forward Planning Unit, COMECE and the CEC Church and Society Commission. We must also mention the interreligious and intercultural dialogue which took place 12-13 February 2002 in Istanbul. This was an initiative of the then Foreign Minister of Turkey, Ismail Cem, who invited politicians from the European Union, EU candidate countries and members of the Organisation of the Islamic Conference (OIC) to attend, representing some 70 countries. The participants affirmed their belief in dialogue among cultures, and condemned terrorist actions in the name of religion. It remains to be seen whether the "spirit of Istanbul", as the then French Foreign Minister Hubert Védrine called it, will advance the interreligious dialogue.

Political institutions can scarcely be moderators of interreligious dialogue. They can offer spaces and possibilities for representatives of different religions to meet, but they should not interfere in the theological area of interreligious dialogue. What they can do is make room for the religions to contribute to the shaping of Europe, and see that this contribution is legally safeguarded. Working together with them is indispensable. President Delors recognised this and created the Working Group "A Soul for Europe", inviting the participation of religious communities and philosophical movements.

The CCEE-CEC Christian-Islamic dialogue as an example of interreligious dialogue

Interreligious dialogue initiatives in Europe are many and diverse. Supranational, regional and national initiative groups, the Focolare Movement, San Egidio, Taizé and others are already making irreplaceable contributions to interreligious dialogue in Europe's churches. Bishops' Conferences and churches have published statements and informational materials, set up working groups and secretariats or appointed persons to be in charge of interreligious dialogue. They have been working along two lines: on one hand helping Christians in their encounters with people of other faiths, and on the other advising Christians in local congregations whose work today is affected by the presence of other religious communities.

In 1978, CEC held a consultation in Salzburg on Islam in Europe. It left many issues open with regard to Islamic theological views and on Christian-Islamic dialogue. The result was that CEC set up an "Islam in Europe" advisory committee, which was to prepare a second consultation to respond to the unanswered questions. This was held in 1984 in St. Pölten, Austria, on the theme "Christian and Muslim Witness to God in a Secular Europe". From the beginning, CCEE was represented in this advisory committee by an observer.

In 1987 CEC and CCEE then set up their Joint Committee on "Islam in Europe". It consists of equal numbers of members of both bodies, and since 1999 has had two moderators. During its first mandate (1987-1991) it worked on "The Presence of Muslims in Europe and the Theological Training of Pastoral Workers". The results of this work were presented to the CEC member churches and the Bishops' Conferences at a conference in Birmingham, England in 1991.

Among the tasks of the Committee's second mandate (1992-1997) were drawing up a guidebook on Christian-Islamic marriages, and reflecting on "reciprocity in Christian-Islamic dialogue". The document on reciprocity was the theme for a meeting with the Christian-Islamic Working Group of the Middle East Council of Churches (MECC). In this working group, Christians and Muslims in the Middle East have been working together for

97

years. Since 1992 it has also been part of the mandate of the "Islam in Europe" Committee that, at its annual business meeting, it meets with representatives of Islamic organisations in the country in which the meeting is held. This enables the committee members to become informed about the situation of Muslims and of dialogue in each such country. For their part, they present the results of their work, or interim reports on it, to the Muslim representatives. The reactions and comments of the Muslims are taken into account in the final editing of information letters and documents.

During its third mandate (1998-2003) the joint "Islam in Europe" Committee has been sending information letters to the churches and Bishops' Conferences on topics in Christian-Muslim dialogue. It is also continuing to work on things to be considered in holding common prayers and rituals during Christian-Muslim encounters, and on a "vade-mecum" booklet for Christian-Muslim dialogue.

In 2001 the Committee took a new initiative by holding a conference, 12-16 September in Sarajevo, Bosnia-Herzegovina, on the theme "Christians and Muslims in Europe: responsibility and religious commitment in a pluralised society", which was attended by over 80 persons from 26 European countries. The incredible massacres of 11 September in New York and Washington the day before the conference opened only prevented a very few people from attending, the reason being that their flights were cancelled. This horrific event was present throughout the conference, being mentioned in welcoming speeches as well as in contributions to the discussions. However, this did not constitute a negative influence on the conference. Instead, the terror attacks had the effect of making the necessity for Christians and Muslims to work together for the good of European society appreciated as more urgent than ever.

This conference in Sarajevo was unprecedented, since the Committee had never organised an event on this scale before, and it was the first such meeting at which Muslims appeared not only as speakers, but also as regular participants in all the work of the conference. The purpose of the conference was for Christian and Muslims, as believers in one God, to reflect together on how to meet their responsibility in the secularised European society of today.

Modern secularism began with the belief that humankind could bring about its own salvation within this world. Science and technology, and political promises of an age of peace and well-being in which human rights are preserved, shape the lives of people in Europe today. This development has also caused religions in Europe to lose their religious and cultural hold over people.

Since 1989 and the fall of the Soviet Union, Communist or socialist ideology has suddenly become much less attractive. The central and eastern European countries have become politically independent and been able to develop democratic structures; within this new political constellation, churches and religious communities have had the possibility of expansion. The transition from Communist atheist dictatorship to secular democracy has not been easy, and the members of faith communities in these countries are still learning to fulfil their political responsibility.

In western European countries, immigration is a cultural and economic fact, but central and eastern European countries are also faced with this reality. The reasons why women and men migrate have to do with economic and political constraints. These waves of immigration, however, have led to a presence of non-Christian religions in Europe which is no longer a marginal phenomenon. That these adherents of other religions, especially large numbers of Muslims, are living in Europe today is a social and political fact. It must be recognised that, through migration, Europe has become visibly multi-religious.

The aim of the conference in Sarajevo was to deal with this situation. Christians and Muslims were to think together about their responsibility in this changed society. They were to draw up models together to show how they could cooperate in the secularised, plural and multi-religious society of today. In their final message they said:

"Together, we wish to contribute to a dynamic identity of our continent, and we advocate a religious attitude which will

- lead us to take courageous actions in favour of human life, freedom, religion, property, dignity and justice;
- give to us and to our faith communities a clear awareness of our common humanity, making us brothers and sisters beyond our different religious and social commitments;
- refuse the justification of violence in the name of religion."

Faith in the one and only God who is confessed by Christians and Muslims together obligates them to work to build up a just society. The "Islam in Europe" Committee wants to make its contribution to doing so, thus carrying out the Christian commitments made in the Charta Oecumenica.

99

Future Prospects

Keith Clements

It is not easy to make predictions, or to advocate directions, for the future of the Charta Oecumenica. Of course, in the shorter term certain things are clear. Both CEC and CCEE as the joint originators of the Charta have an equal responsibility to ensure a proper evaluation and reflection upon the text and its reception thus far, at their respective assemblies in 2003. It is open to their supreme governing bodies to decide what further steps should be taken in refinement, revision or development of the document - or to decide to leave it alone and allow the reception process of the text as it stands to continue among the Churches of Europe.

What makes prediction and advocacy an uncertain exercise, however, is that the Charta and its reception process have already taken on a life of their own, and already that life has produced results quite unexpected when it was signed by the Presidents of CEC and CCEE at Strasbourg in April 2001. It is like a seed which produces blooms much more variegated and therefore much more interesting than what was envisaged by the sower. It has provided not just a text, but a context, of language, direction and vision in which Churches, groups and individuals can locate their specific ecumenical commitments. At a time when many have been saying that the ecumenical movement is dying if not dead, it has provided the European Churches with a newly constructed common framework of basic orientations and encouragement for pursuit of the goal of deeper cooperation and indeed a commitment to seek visible unity. Quite apart, then, from what CEC and CCEE might decide to do for its future, the life-to-be of the Charta is inseparable from what the Churches of Europe decide on for their future progress towards unity - or indeed what events may surprise, challenge and overtake the Churches themselves. Future prospects for the Charta are therefore bound up with what issues and developments one can foresee for the European ecumenical enterprise as a whole.

The question therefore is, what interactions might we expect between the commitments laid down in the Charta and the foreseeable developments in European Christianity in the coming years? There is not space here to proceed in turn through all the paragraphs of the text, but let us select some highlights.

Towards visible unity?

First, Section I which recapitulates the basis of ecumenical endeavour as centred in belief in "One Holy, Catholic and Apostolic Church" includes the commitment: "in the power of the Holy Spirit, to work towards the visible unity of the Church of Jesus Christ, expressed in the mutual recognition of baptism and in eucharistic fellowship, as well as in common witness and service." Likewise Section II lays down quite clearly the commitment "to move towards the goal of eucharistic fellowship." This is a mighty commitment to make, and if indeed it is a commitment and not just an idle wish or dreamy hope it has quite cataclysmic implications for the present state of inter-church relations at certain levels. Let us be quite frank: certain official Church statements in the very recent past have been more concerned to state reasons against rather than for intercommunion or even "eucharistic hospitality." But to be equally frank, it has to be honestly recognized that, irrespective of the carefully formulated theological pronouncements of Church hierarchies and official bodies, more and more of the actual membership of the Churches, the laos of God, are making up their own minds on this issue. They simply cannot see, for example, why those whom God has joined together in holy matrimony should be separated at the table of the Lord who died to make "a single new humanity" (Ephesians 2.15). Or they refuse to believe that those who at local community level from Monday to Saturday live together, struggle together and suffer together in the "liturgy after the liturgy" of witnessing to God's peace and justice in the world should then tolerate ecclesiastical barriers to their communion in holy bread and wine on Sundays. To say this is not to take up a particular position for or against the official practices of Churches at present. It is simply to address the fact that, like it or not, certain far-reaching developments are taking place in the actual life of our Churches with which official theologies will eventually have to come to terms. The commitments from the Charta quoted above plunge us all into the heart of this issue, not least because they place themselves "in the power of the Holy Spirit" - and who is to determine or limit when and where that power is in operation? As the Charta itself states in respect of "fundamental differences in faith" still being barriers to unity - different views of the church, sacraments and ministries etc - "We must not be satisfied with this situation." As such, the Charta therefore legitimates much further stormy debate within and between the Churches. To put it another way round, we can expect the Charta to be drawn into and cited in these debates which we are probably only just beginning to engage with seriously.

The future of the Charta must also be seen in the context of the current and continuing debate about the nature of the visible unity which is to be sought, and therewith the path towards it. At the risk of greatly oversimplifying, one can summarise a good deal of recent "Faith and Order" debate on ecumenical goals and methodologies as lying between, on the one hand, reaching agreement or consensus on doctrinal questions, and on the other hand as entry into a relational enterprise whereby Churches seek not so much propositional agreement as a dynamic koinonia, communion or fellowship which permits "reconciled diversity." What is interesting about the Charta in this regard is that it commits the Churches to a new level of relational life, deepening cooperation and fellowship at every level, while recognising that "fundamental differences" still call for resolution. Through the Charta, the European Churches are in effect turning themselves into a kind of laboratory of ecumenical experiment, the results of which cannot really be foreseen. If they go down this road of commitment to inter-relationship, will that of itself enable them to solve all the "fundamental differences", or provide a new perspective in light of which hitherto undreamt of solutions emerge? Or will it, as some imagine, enable those differences to be set aside? Or will they eventually still "hit the wall" like the marathon runner who finds that no amount of training is adequate to cope with the last few kilometres of the race and has to rely on will-power alone? For this reason, if no other, it is important that the future life and utilisation of the Charta be not only monitored by CEC and CCEE but shared with the wider ecumenical community for example through the WCC Faith and Order Commission, as a test-case with vital import for the overall quest for visible unity.

Unity in mission

Second, the future life and role of the Charta Oecumenica are bound up with the burgeoning consciousness in the European Churches of their missionary role in Europe. Significantly, the responses of the Churches to the first draft of the Charta during 1999-2000 cited almost more frequently than anything else the need for a more emphatic assertion of mission and evangelism as a primary commitment today. It is for this reason that in the revised text Section II now opens with the declaration "The most important task of the churches in Europe is the common proclamation of the Gospel, in both word and deed, for the salvation of all" and calls for the whole people of God together to communicate the Gospel in the public domain. Today, any talk of "Christian Europe" requires much qualification. By the same token, any one single characterisation of contemporary Europe is much too superficial and glib, whether "secular", "post-modern", "post-Christian" or even "pluralist" (since the plurality itself takes a variety of forms depending on where exactly one is talking about!). In fact one of the good things in our contemporary scene is the renewed debate about the relationship of the Churches, and religion generally, to society and culture. Even, it is being asked, was Europe ever "really Christian" and if so in what sense? We can expect this debate to grow in intensity and to affect progressively all the Churches. The debate will be set between several poles. There will, for example, be those who in effect will say that all that needs to be done is to remind Europe of its Christian roots and people will sooner or later give up on their flirtations with eastern religions or New Ageism or sheer secularism, and flock back to Mother Church; while on the other hand there will be those who feel that European culture (in its western forms at any rate) is now so deeply sunk in its apostasy of rationalism, materialism and individualism that it is inherently and inimically hostile to the Gospel. Both poles are too simplistic in their respective optimism and despair. Like all cultures with which the Gospel has engaged in the story of Christian mission down the ages, contemporary Europe is a complex mixture of "Gospel-friendly" and "Gospel-unfriendly" elements.

The Charta is important here because it recalls the Churches to focus first on the Gospel itself and their calling to proclaim it, and not first to examine how far Europe is receptive to it or otherwise, or how far the traditional role of the churches as religious institutions can be maintained. Only Churches which have a primary confidence in the message of Jesus Christ and in the communicative power of the Holy Spirit have any future in Europe. Only Churches which are not first of all concerned with maintaining their historic position and influence (real or imagined) in society, but seek first of all to be genuinely missionary churches, will in the providence of God and in reality come to have any position and influence worth having. Only Churches which seek first the reign of God and God's justice will find that all the other necessary things will be added to them (Matthew 6.33). On the basis of a genuinely evangelical confidence and seriousness (and joy!) the Churches are then free to examine and experiment how the Gospel can by turns affirm, confront, challenge, accompany, provide space for, contemporary Europeans in their search for the meaning of life. They are also enabled and liberated, as a matter of course, as the Charta puts it, "to overcome the feeling of self-sufficiency within each church" and to seek help, education and enrichment from each other in their common task of evangelism.

A crucial test of the churches' commitment in this area, and of how seriously they take the Charta, will be their readiness to have their actions, very concretely and specifically, measured against what the Charta calls for in this section. Nowhere is this more pertinent than in the first commitment tabled in Section II: "to discuss our plans for evangelisation with other churches, entering into agreements with them and thus avoiding harmful competition and the risk of fresh divisions." To be very concrete and specific in the context of a present controversy, what does this say for instance to the present dispute between the Roman Catholic Church and the Russian Orthodox Church over the issue of new Roman Catholic dioceses in Russia? What is said in the Charta and what is actually happening in such mutually painful episodes simply must be exposed to each other if the Charta is to have any real credibility. Or put the other way round, if the Charta is ignored or not taken seriously and such conflicts are not confronted with the call to reconciliation, then it is the credibility of the Gospel itself which is at stake in the world today. The Charta is a tool which can be sharpened and increased in its effectiveness only as it is hammered against the hard rocks of our contemporary life. Better for it to risk being broken in that engagement, than slowly to rust away on a shelf supposedly out of harm's way. All this of course puts another question to us as we contemplate the future of the Charta: what means do we have in CEC and CCEE actually to assess whether it is being implemented or not? Those who raised questions in the earlier part of the process, about how far the Charta is "binding" or in some sense "legislative" for the Churches do at least have a real point. Affirmation of the Charta by any Church carries with it the implicit willingness to be held accountable to it - but by whom and under what authority? In creating the Charta we have posed for ourselves major questions further down the line. They are questions which some may have thought (or hoped) to have been laid to rest with the apparent demise of the conciliar process of covenanting for "Justice, Peace and the Integrity of Creation."

These questions are now resurrecting themselves, and not least to CEC and CCEE as such. The Charta states: "At the European level it is necessary to strengthen co-operation between the Conference of European Churches and the Council of European Bishops' Conferences (CCEE) and to hold further European Ecumenical Assemblies." Cruising just below the surface of such a statement, however, is the persistent question of whether strengthened cooperation between CEC and CCEE will itself be adequate to maintain the vision and aims of the Charta Oecumenica and its requirements of implementation and accountability. For some time there have already been voices asking why CEC and CCEE exist apart from each other. How much longer can we in Europe (in contrast for example to the Middle East and the Caribbean) continue without a truly ecumenical body wholly inclusive of the Roman Catholic Church as well as all others?

But the question of inclusiveness does not end just there. The Charta Oecumenica, being a product of CEC and CCEE, owes itself largely to what are (in their own self-description) the "mainline" Churches of Europe: that is, those which historically arose in Europe and which regard themselves - irrespective of their numerical size or relationships with the state or their status whether as "national" or "free" churches - as the indigenous forms of European Christianity. The map and landscape of European Christianity are, however, changing fast. Especially important as a factor in these changes is the growing and increasingly significant presence of so-called diaspora Churches, particularly from Africa and Asia. Immigration into Europe from the "south" and its Christian communities is fast becoming as important a fact of Christian history as was the European exportation of Christianity to those continents through colonialism and missionary enterprise over the last two centuries. Korean Presbyterian congregations are making their presence felt in many European cities. African worshipping communities in many European countries are challenging the seemingly defeatist ethos of our "mainline" churches in face of secularism, with a vibrant missionary zeal as socially conscious as it is evangelistic. A truly ecumenical European Christianity must be open to this presence and the challenge and enrichment which it brings, at every level - local, national, regional and pan-European. For their part, the "mainline" Churches cannot at one and the same time claim to be open to the leading of the Holy Spirit and presume to deny to these newer arrivals on the scene a genuine commonality within the European Christian family. They are now part of the European scene. And the Charta Oecumenica, precisely by its broad and generous terminology about the calling of all the European Churches to mission in their own continent, can be a powerful tool for encouraging and building this wider ecumenical missionary consciousness. It should hardly be necessary to add that the Charta can and will be invoked in the continuing debates about "common prayer", coming to terms with the past, and the requirement to continue in dialogue.

European unity and common responsibility

Third, in its stated commitment of the Churches to the integration of Europe (Section III) the Charta Oecumenica provides a much needed compass for setting the course and direction for the Churches in the coming few years which will take Europe into uncharted and possibly stormy waters. At the present time we are at a crucial moment in the social, economic and political development of Europe. The European Convention process which has invited debate on the future of the European Union not only among governments but also with many actors in civil society including the Churches, will culminate in 2004 in far-reaching decisions on the size and shape of the EU. The lives of all Europeans will be affected, not only in EU-member states, not only in applicant countries, but also in countries which for a long time or perhaps never will be part of the EU. The most that can be said is that nothing is certain. It may be that enlargement will take place relatively smoothly. It could also prove to be a very divisive process: dividing countries within the EU into a rich and powerful core and a lower league of second-class members. It might even see a secession by some members. Whatever happens, we could see a new division of Europe along economic lines with a protective curtain against those outside, and the risk of further destabilisation in the east. Highly significant then is the Charta's statement: "As churches and as international communities we have to counteract the danger of Europe developing into an integrated West and a disintegrated East, and also take account of the North-South divide within Europe. At the same time we must avoid Eurocentricity and heighten Europe's sense of responsibility for the whole of humanity, particularly for the poor all over the world."

It is in this section dealing with our common responsibility in Europe, that the stated nature of the Charta Oecumenica as a "basis text" becomes especially apparent. The basic parameters for that common responsibility are quite clear: commitment to a Europe based on unifying values of justice,

106

peace, the dignity of the human person, democratisation, the just treatment and welfare of migrants, refugees and asylum seekers, and the safeguarding of the creation. At the same time, it may well prove that in the coming years particular issues may arise which will require more specific responses by the Churches either in part or the whole of Europe. That may well mean extension or in-filling of the present Charta. Nowhere is this more important than in the commitment "to work for structures of peace, based on the non-violent resolution of conflicts." The commitment to work for structures of peace is itself a daunting challenge which is hardly as yet on our Churches' or ecumenical bodies' agendas in any meaningful way. But just supposing that the Churches, with or without cooperation with other groups, were to set out a programme or mechanism for non-violent conflict resolution and seek its proper resourcing, it would merit and require a serious and solemn declaration by the Churches that they support it as a necessary component of their faith and mission, an element in a further Charta Oecumenica Pro Pacem Europae et Mundi.

The same can be said of the commitments in inter-faith relations, the area which is so fast growing in urgency. It is tempting for us to speculate on how chapter 11, "Cultivating relations with Islam" might have been re-phrased had the events of 11 September 2001 occurred before, instead of five months after, the signing of the Charta. In fact the sobriety and restraint - some feel even understatement - of these paragraphs probably suits the new situation better than any emotionally charged and agonised rhetoric would have done. It is enough - demanding enough and potentially fruitful enough - to call for intensifying Christian-Islamic dialogue at all levels, to conduct ourselves towards Muslims "with respect," and to work together with them on matters of common concern. We may well find it possible and necessary to say more than this (as on relationships with Judaism) in the future but if so it will only be because we have concentrated on following through these basic first steps. How tempting it would have been immediately after 11 September, to have declared (with an appropriate Biblical and perhaps even Koranic flourish) that we recognize violence to be inimical to both the Christian and Muslim traditions. That would have been an attempt, too soon, to evade the uncomfortable questions about the violent elements which have intertwined themselves into the actual histories of both traditions down the centuries. It would have been an instant anaesthetic to cover the pain rather than giving time and space for an adequate diagnosis. Better to begin with respectful dialogue than indulgent oratory. The issues lying between "the world of Islam" and "the West" are highly complex and are going to tax us exceedingly for the near future at least. We shall find ourselves being grateful that the Charta did not try to say too much but indicated the beginning of the journey and the direction to be followed. But perhaps we can envisage, eventually, nothing less than a Charta on the growing cooperation of Christians and Muslims in Europe - produced by both faith traditions together. And perhaps an even wider multi-faith text which, like the Charta Oecumenica, would not just be a declaration of religious leaders but prepared over a period of time and involving discussion and contributions from faith-communities at every level.

So then ...

It is clear that CEC and CCEE together will have to consider what means - and their resourcing - will be appropriate to monitor, accompany and guide the future course of the Charta Oecumenica, the responses it will provoke, the new encounters and initiatives it will stimulate, the dialogues and experiments it will facilitate, at every level. Moreover, we may well need others to help us in that task, because a further development in the story of the Charta is already apparent: its transmission to churches and ecumenical bodies outside Europe and the interest being taken in it by our partners in far places. We have started something which in its early stages has already surprised us, and more surprises may well be in store. How apposite it was, then, to place as the concluding words of the Charta the prayer of the Apostle Paul "that we may abound in hope by the power of the Holy Spirit."

BIOGRAPHICAL INFORMATION
ON AUTHORS

Keith Clements

Born 1943. Minister of the Baptist Union of Great Britain. 1967-77, pastor of local congregations. 1977-1990, Lecturer, Bristol Baptist College and Department of Theology and Religious Studies, University of Bristol. 1990-97 Secretary for International Affairs, Council of Churches for Britain and Ireland. Since 1997 General Secretary, Conference of European Churches, Geneva. Author of works on modern church history and the ecumenical movement.

John Coughlan

Works for the Commission of the Bishops' Conferences of the European Community (COMECE) in Brussels, responsible for relations with the media and foreign policy issues. Editor of the monthly review Europe Infos. Born in Wales to Irish and Scots parents and educated at the University of Oxford, England.

Reinhard Frieling

Evangelical Church in Germany; Moderator of the Europe Committee of the EKD Synod; Moderator of the CEC Commission "Churches in Dialogue"; Director of the Konfessionskundliches Institut Bensheim (1981-1999). At present Honorary Professor for Ecumenical Theology at the Evangelical Theological Faculty, Marburg, Germany.

Aldo Giordano

Born 1954 in Italy, Roman Catholic priest from the diocese of Cuneo. Theological studies in Fossano (Cuneo) and philosophy at the Gregorian University in Rome. His research and essays deal particularly with ethics and contemporary philosophy. Since 1995 General Secretary of the Council of European Bishops' Conferences (CCEE).

Waclaw Hryniewicz

Professor, since 1983 head of the department of Eastern theology at the Ecumenical Institute of the Catholic University of Lublin; since 1997 director of this Institute; since 1980 member of the Joint International Commission for Theological Dialogue between the Roman Catholic Church and the Orthodox Church; author of more than 20 books on paschal theology, hope, eschatology, Old-Russian theology and ecumenism.

Viorel Ionita

Born in 1945. Priest of the Romanian Orthodox Church; Professor at the Orthodox Theological Faculty of the University Bucharest, Romania and simultaneously Study Secretary of CEC. Responsible for the work on the Charta Oecumenica on the CEC side.

Keith Jenkins

1981-1986, Secretary of the British Council of Churches' Race Relations Unit (BCC); 1982-1987, Member of the Board of the Churches' Commission for Migrants in Europe (CCME); 1986-1990, Assistant General Secretary of the British Council of Churches (BCC); 1990-1998, General Secretary of the Ecumenical Commission for Church and Society (EECCS); 1998-2002, Director of the Church and Society Commission of CEC and Associate General Secretary of CEC.

Metropolitan Jérémie of Switzerland

Born 1935 in Kos, Greece. Theological studies in Patmos, Chalki-Constantinople and at the Sorbonne, Paris. 1964 ordained as priest and 1971 as Bishop (of Sasima), Metropolitan of France from 1988-2003, at present Metropolitan of Switzerland. Since the Assembly in 1979 member of the different ecumenical commissions of CEC and president of CEC since 1997.

Heinz Klautke

German Protestant pastor, born 1937, lived and worked as pastor for the German speaking Protestant congregation in Turkey from 1975 to 1987; afterwards Secretary for Islam relations of the Evangelical Church in Germany (1987-2001); co-moderator of the "Islam in Europe" Committee of CEC and CCEE, now retired, lives in Hannover, Germany.

Grigorios Larentzakis

Orthodox theological studies at Chalki (Constantinople) and Thessaloniki. PhD in Theology in 1983. Catholic theological studies in

Salzburg and Innsbruck, PhD in Catholic Theology 1969. Teaching Orthodox and Ecumenical Theology in Graz (since 1970). Head of the Department for Theology of the Eastern Orthodox Churches. Member of the Central Committee of the Conference of European Churches and the Commission "Churches in Dialogue". Many publications in various languages.

Sarah Numico

Born in Italy in 1970, graduated in Slavic literature and philosophy. From 1995-1997 national President of the Federation of Catholic University Students in Italy (FUCI). Since 1998 staff member of the Council of European Bishops' Conferences, currently as press officer. Coordinator for the organisation of the European Ecumenical Encounter of Strasbourg, 2001 for CCEE.

Petra Pajdakovic

Student of theology, Catholic Theological Faculty, University of Zagreb, Croatia; youth and student activist, experienced in Christian journalism. Since 2001 member of the Ecumenism and Dialogue Committee of the Croatian Bishops' Conference; acting Regional Coordinator for inter-religious dialogue programs in the Balkans of Pax Christi Netherlands.

Hans Vöcking Afr.M.

Studies of Philosophy (Trier), Theology (Louvain) and of Islam (Rome). Director of the Centre of social and economic documentation in Oran (Algeria) 1973-1979, Head of CIBEDO (Christian-Islamic Centre for Encounter and Documentation), Frankfurt, 1979-1998, Lecturer at the Papal Institute for Arabic, and expert on Islam. Associated staff of CCEE in the fields of Islam and Migration.